ZERO DEBT
ZERO STRESS

The happiness of having a future filled with love and wealth.

A practical and effective method to help you get out of debt.

Paul Evens CHERY

Copyright © 2018 by Paul Evens CHERY

All rights reserved.

ISBN : 9781981073894

TABLE OF CONTENTS

Dedication

Introduction

PART 1

My Current Situation

Chapter 1 – An erroneous daily life...13

Chapter 2 – My meeting with the angel..17

PART 2

Get Out Of Ignorance

Chapter 3 - Debt..23

Chapter 4 – Leverage..31

Chapter 5 - Stress..35

Chapter 6 – Financial Stress...41

Chapter 7 - Money..47

Chapter 8 – Love...67

Chapter 9 - Friendship..85

Chapter 10 – Family..97

Chapter 11 - Procrastination..103

Chapter 12 - Entrepreneurship..115

Chapter 13 – Investment..125

PART 3

The Four (4) Key Steps to Getting Out of Debt

Chapter 14 - Step # 1 : Be Healthy..141

Chapter 15 - Step # 2 : Find Happiness.......................................149

Chapter 16 - Step # 3 : Give and Receive....................................167

Chapter 17 - Step # 4 : Become Financially Free.......................195

DEDICATION

First, I thank God who took me as an instrument to bring this message. To my dear wife Feeding Adelson CHERY, for her moral support during the writing of this book. To my parents for their sacrifice and for putting me on this way. To my sisters for their support. And especially to my cousin Jean Charles for his contribution to my university education.

INTRODUCTION

Many people, businesses, states are crumbling under debt. Today, the great apparatus of the economy is automated by debt. We all live on credit. State expenditures are settled by borrowing.

Debt has become the undisputed fuel of the economy, and the engine of global growth. We are all caught in the gear of an economic machine that makes day by day always more debt. And this machine has become packed, it has become uncertain and the public debt (the debt of the states) is exploding.

The pressure of society, of advertising influences our needs to possess at all costs. Branded clothing, the "I's" of the apple, the latest game console ... "Buy now and pay later"; we are therefore easy prey for credit companies and traders.

Many people are trapped by the effects of advertising that make products "indispensable" to exist.

And when you do not master the dynamics of your debts, it's very difficult to get out. From a certain level of indebtedness, we are caught in a spiral. To pay off debt and interest, we have no choice but to borrow more and more.

Young people rarely go into debt for more or less eligible causes. Some blow up their phone bills by exaggerating the options of their packages; others overload their credit cards, often two or more! With spontaneous purchases; and many rely on the generosity of their landlord by accumulating late rent payments. Managing their finances is not a privilege.

Until the collection agencies start calling them and knocking on their door they grasp the gravity of the situation, but it is often too late.

Easy access to credit encourages young buyers to provide more credit and debt without even realizing it. A purchase here and there is soon changing into dozens of bills on credit which weigh heavily on their bank statement and on their shoulders.

Consumer debts have a bad effect on the quality of life by raising the level of stress, anxiety and bouts of insomnia. Many people are now turning to antidepressants to deal with this situation, and others who do not know how to cope, want to commit suicide.

These physical and mental health problems derive from this financial stress that turns daily life into an illusion.

Before the 1960s, the use of credit to make ordinary purchases was a very rare fact. Public opinion was unfavorable because consumer credit was associated with a horrible administration of personal affairs. Today, things have changed a lot. Consumer credit is now part of the daily lifestyle.

Thanks to credit, we are not forced to delay the fulfillment of certain desires such as the acquisition of a car, for example.

Every day, faced with the events of life, we appreciate, we endure, our unconscious perceives indications that raise questions about our function in destiny.

The task of our unconscious, especially through the dream. Erected from scratch from a word, a sentence, a character related to the incidents we have just experienced.

In Egypt, the libraries called "The Treasure of the Remedies of the Soul" because it cured the worst of evils: Ignorance.

Ignorance is a shameful, dangerous state, and the grave reason for this ignorance is pride.

Pride is an incessant danger. Knowledge is obtained first by means of the human intellect and can thus be engraved more or less in our memory. Knowledge can apply to our heart and our consciousness.

But if our knowledge remains simply on a question of intelligence, it remains without result on our internal being and can even lead to a feeling of pride and an alleged superiority towards others.

Many people miss out on opportunities, do not fully grasp their heritage, and do not enjoy much of the love and wealth because they are devoid of knowledge.

When we ignore something, we cannot enjoy the benefits and benefits of knowing that thing. The person who knows who he is, will have the power, confidence and pride to deal with any situation.

PAUL EVENS CHERY

PART 1

MY CURRENT SITUATION

CHAPTER 1

AN ERRONEOUS DAILY LIFE

Dmitri Selbant, lived in a small town in Russia. He worked as a bookkeeper in a technology company since 5 years. His parents lived in the countryside, but to make things easier, he rented a small apartment downtown to better access his job.

He lived far beyond his means; his salary could not really cover his basic needs. He tried several requests for increase and promotion, but unfortunately in vain.

The unemployment rate in the region was so high that it seemed impossible to consider a job change. In this sense, Dmitri should do with it. To cover his budget deficit, he had to obtain credit cards at several financial institutions in the city. In the end, he became the holder of six (6) credit cards, which made it difficult for him to pay the minimum of his cards.

Dmitri felt confused, upset, he could not sleep at night, he was constantly thinking about remedying the situation. So he resolved to eliminate all his debts and reset the counter. Because of this, he decided to go see Jason Cooper, the owner of a business house in the area to ask him a big loan. This man was also recognized as a member of the Russian Mafia.

That morning, Selbant woke up with a cheerful face, the azure sky stretched as far as the eye could see, the rays of the sun warming the earth and transforming the fields into the golden sea, had become the day he should meet Cooper.

So he got up from his bed and went to take a bath, not even wanting to eat anything, and fled to the Jason Cooper business house very early. It was around 7:55 am when he arrived, and just Tony, Mr. Cooper's bodyguard was going to open the business.

- Selbant approached Tony all disturbing - "Hello sir"

- *Hello sir, how can I help you?* He asked him with a bad look.

- *My name is Dmitri, I would like to meet Mr Jason Cooper ".*

- *Did you have an appointment with Mr Cooper?"* Tony

- *No, but I certainly want to see him today,* "replied Dmitri.

- *"You can come in and wait here,"* Tony said.

A few minutes later, Tony comes back and tells him - *Please go ahead, Mr. Cooper is waiting for you in his office.*

- *Hello Mr. Cooper, my name is Dmitri Selbant, It's a great honor for me to receive me in your office this morning"* while smiling.

- *Cooper answers him, and say, sit down, what can I do for you?*

- *Dmitri: I have a small money problem. I told a friend about it, and he advised me to come and see you so that you could borrow a little.*

- *Cooper: You have to pay me every month.*

- Dmitri : *Yes, it is OK.*

Cooper opens a drawer in his office and hands the money over to Dmitri after signing a debt promise.

Dmitri takes the money, thanks Cooper, and left. Obviously, Dmitri goes and pays all her debts.

He paid Cooper every month as promised. After five months, he felt good with this little debt, he started to party with his friends more often, just as before. And there, his expenses increase and his savings start to suffocate.

One day on the road for work, Dmitri had an accident and he remained in coma for a few days.

CHAPTER 2

MY MEETING WITH ANGEL

- *Dmitri, Dmitri, Dmitri,* exclaims a soft voice.

And suddenly, Dmitri wakes up, and here he is at the edge of a river, in the middle of a beautiful garden of flowers.

When he looks behind him, he sees a beautiful creature dressed in white, and a light shining on her and on her face.

- She says: Hi Dmitri.

- Dmitri answers: Who are you? And where are we?

- With a small smile on her lips, she said to Dmitri: *My name is Vester; I am the angel of the Human Consciousness. My mission is to bring light to every person living on earth. I have always spoken to you every day, but you have never given importance to my word, you have always chosen your line, you choose to do what others tell you.*

- Dmitri: *No. This is the first time I see you.*

- Vester: "I'm in the head of every human creature, I usually talk to you through your subconscious to clarify for you something you do not understand, and sometimes I talk to you when you sleep through pictures to explain certain things to you. But often you forget them, because you give more importance to the words of others. What do you think you do here?

- Dmitri: *I'm dead and now I'm in paradise.*

- Vester laughs, and says: *you are not dead. I put your body somewhere and take you to another world, where people can not disturb you so that I can help you understand some things that are so important to you, that will allow you to live better by being on the earth. You were born in a poor family, your biggest dream was to have a comfortable life and contribute to the well-being of your parents. But your ways are bad. Your father is dead and you did not do anything for him. And if you continue like this, your mother will die in misery and you too.*

- Dmitri smiled and asked him: So, are you going to make me rich very fast?

- The angel answers: *A faithful person will be richly blessed, but one eager to get rich will not go unpunished. Do not wear yourself out to get rich; do not trust your own cleverness. Cast but a glance at riches, and they are gone, for they will surely sprout wings and fly off to the sky like an eagle. I will give you the steps to follow so that you can become rich and live happily. But you are free to take another way. That's why God created you with free will to make the decisions you want. She asks Dmitri, do you want to start learning?*

- Dmitri answers: *Yes, I am ready.*

- Vester: *I already gave you everything, you wrote them with your own hand, but it was me who dictated to you through your subconscious.*

- Dmitri: *I have a notebook filled with meaningless things that I wrote without thinking about it. Is that it?*

- Vester: *Yes, you did not understand them, because it was not your own words. Go now, read them, try to understand them and put them into practice and you will live better.*

PART 2

GET OUT OF IGNORANCE

CHAPTER 3

DEBT

The rich rule over the poor, and the borrower is slave to the lender.

Indebtedness indicates a situation marked by the accumulation of debts, sums that a person is required to repay.

Indebtedness refers to an accumulation of non-surrendered money borrowing. Indebtedness can lead to stress, especially fatal for the client's health. In addition, indebtedness can lead to psychological breakdown and social isolation.

Also, financial problems associated with indebtedness are usually a source of conflict, and even separation, in couples.

The over-indebtedness responds to a situation of financial fatality that blocks someone from facing all of their debts.

This is defined by the impossibility of covering both his daily expenses and the payment of his debts. As a result, you will not be able to cope with your bills or your payment expirations and just survive financially.

It is said that there is over-indebtedness when the situation continues and ends up revealing impracticable.

There is nothing more exhausting than holding debts. To optimize its financial situation, we will have to take this very seriously, and act quickly, especially in a crisis phase where the unemployment rate is constantly rising.

There is always a strategy to put in place, however do not wait to react.

By adopting the right rules and getting used to managing your budget, overindebtedness is not a calamity. But assistance to pay off debts is a prerogative.

Before embracing any maneuver, first draw up the account of the situation. Make a list and add what you pocket, your monthly disbursements, and finally, everything you owe and your creditors. This will help you first to have an overview that will allow you to determine the next step.

After, try to record all the expenses that would have occurred in the coming months. By having a representation of future expenses, you can more naturally prepare a program of assistance to repay your debts as soon as possible.

We must first make an assessment of everything we need, to be able to assess its willingness to pay in the time granted. And set an order of priority in the payment if it is not easy to consider them all at once.

You will have to make cuts in your budget, unless you have exceptional revenues. As a result, likewise for its list of debts, it is necessary to list its monthly exchanges and to see those from which one can cut oneself off.

One can also try to renegotiate with its suppliers, to switch insurance if it is excessively expensive, review its telephone plan, save energy, separate unnecessary expenses.

The budget allows you to highlight your finances. You will understand how much you receive, how much you have to pay and you will be able to arrange your payments accordingly. With a budget, he is much freer to administer his money.

Now that you have specified to whom and how much you owe, contact each of your donors and let them understand the situation. In many cases, you simply need to lower your monthly payments or stop for a limited time the repayment of a debt.

Talking with your creditors first helps you build a relationship of trust that will persuade them of your loyalty to your willingness to pay, and then help you discover together assistance to pay off your debts and a plan for distributing your repayments.

When you have control of the situation, restructure your expenses.

Determine a monthly amount by seeing wide to make sure you are in the nails. In this way, if you have a little more money at the end of the period, you can either pay a larger amount on one of your debts, or save it for hard times.

Similarly, eliminate wasteful expenses. Each of these small savings will help you enormously in the future.

To limit oneself is not always simple. However it is imperative to continue your efforts in order to get out of debt.

Review your account from time to time: check your expenses and compare them with the budget you set up. Keep in touch with your creditor who you depend on to maintain a good relationship.

It will help you to recover and see some mistakes, but also to get out of debt as soon as possible.

You must react quickly, as debts will increase and influence family life vigorously. The main thing to put in place is to examine well before accepting a credit, and not listening to one's desires.

When you get something, ask yourself if you really need it and if you can pay cash. Stop paying by credit because you will be more involved in debt.

Between the acquisition of a good with a credit the acquisition of the same good in a single cash payment, the differentiations manage to mix so that the price of a good ends to be hidden by the amount of the monthly payments.

A well-established loan program can help administer your debts. You can also prevent them by managing your expenses and your savings carefully.

Nevertheless, you will spend periods in your life where you will have to borrow money.

So, why not look at the best way to borrow smartly and the best way to pay those debts in a reasonable and concrete way.

Initially, you need to determine if you see the thing you are borrowing as good or bad debt. Going into debt for a need or something that will increase in value over time, however, seems appropriate.

You must know that the acquisition of a building is not a trap that you cannot get rid of. If you buy a home that has the right repayments, you can expect that its value will increase for later sale.

The profits thus obtained by this business will help you to buy a more expensive house.

Credit is a useful and sometimes indispensable tool. However, credit prescribes debts that are often hard to pay. And worst of all, credit creates a false sense of happiness that can lead to over-indebtedness.

Self-control or self-control is the ability to control one's emotions and not move forward without previously examining the situation.

Someone who is unable to do so chooses a spontaneous attitude. Spontaneity is a character trait that excites an individual to walk without questioning the impulsive aspects of the action.

If self-control is essential to prevent a condition of over-indebtedness, it is clear that the socio-economic environment as long as the sociodemographic characteristics of an individual also play on his fragility in this situation.

Debt is not always a bad thing. One can make a fortune with debts, thanks to the leverage in real estate, among others.

CHAPTER 4

LEVERAGE

Leverage indicates the opportunity to use financing to increase profits, thereby raising risks.

Leverage refers to the fact that a company uses indebtedness to try to improve the profitability of its equity. It measures the interest of this institution to solicit financing from others, particularly in the form of bank credit, given the current profitability of its equity. The goal is that the result of the funded project is greater than the amount of funding for its project.

The leverage is then qualified as positive. If the cost of the project is greater than its profitability, it will thus disadvantage the return on equity.

Leverage is used to indicate any style that aims to maximize profits, but also losses.

The loan helps to acquire assets or invest with a minimum of equity.

If the rate of return on the asset is above the credit rate, the leverage is positive. Debt thus makes it possible to increase the return on equity.

If the rate of return on the asset is lower than the financing rate, the leverage is negative. The cost of borrowing comes at a disadvantage to the return on equity. So we speak of boomerang.

Leverage helps to increase the movement of a market, mobilizing only a fraction of the real amount of your investment.

To calculate the leverage, you only need to know two variables: The nominal value of your position and the required coverage.

The nominal value of your position is the actual amount invested in the market.

Leverage gives you the benefit of outperforming the market. By amplifying the movements of the market, it is advisable to follow your positions carefully, focusing on short-term strategies.

If your winnings can be significant in the event of adverse market developments, your losses may exceed your initial investment and you must replenish your account if you want to maintain your position.

Leverage helps to measure the importance of using bank financing or from third parties. It is a powerful tool to enable capital holders to obtain high financial productivity.

However, the more serious the lever is used, the more the boomerang effect can be dangerous.

CHAPTER 5

STRESS

Our pace of life is much more intense today than it was a few years ago. Nobody can avoid stress and tension in everyday life.

In our modern, performance-oriented society, stress is part of everyday life for many people.

What is stress?

Stress is often defined as the inability to cope with a destabilizing situation, most of the time because it is new and we do not know how to apprehend it. In the body, a whole mechanism is then set in motion to optimize vigilance and concentration, to allow you to better adapt to this new situation.

Stress is a reflex of natural safeguarding of the body in the face of a difficult situation.

To facilitate the reaction, the body produces adrenaline that increases the heart rate, accelerates breathing and gives a boost of energy.

Stress can be very useful in a condition requiring a prompt response or a particularly important effort. Clearly, too much stress is not good.

Stress indicates the psychological device implemented by the body to cope with a mainly painful condition.

It is also a set of reflexes of the body when this is dominated by constraints. Stress can appear from any aggression, whether it is an infection, an organic pathology, a withdrawn symptom, or a psychiatric difficulty.

Stress can catch anyone from time to time or sometimes daily turning into a real handicap in everyday life.

Stress responds to reactions of the nascent body as soon as the organism is in the presence of a violent change of situation. The body organism reacts against what it perceives an aggression or a constraint.

Each person reacts in a particular way and adjusted to an incident which he sees as shocking. Stress is usually consistent with pressures caused by unresolved clean fights.

Prolonged stress can lead to psychological and physical exhaustion. Stress can be a cause causing various pathologies, such as cardiovascular diseases, eczema, migraine...

Work-related stress is the leading cause of sickness. The term overwork and burn out is often used.

The stress causes an imbalance of the nervous system: it incites the hypotalamo-pituitary and adrenal nervous system.

Stress can be ephemeral and appear in isolation. Stress can also continue periodically and completely paralyze daily life.

How to stay calm and relaxed despite the stress?

The World Health Organization (WHO) produces studies on stress that shows that this is a major issue valid on all continents, which is concerned in automatic the world, the worker as well as the framework, the student as much as the inactive ones.

Everyone at his level shows signs of fatigue and tensions generated by stress. Collateral damage can be significant when living with sometimes daily or permanent pressure.

Everyone may not have the chance to decompress. In the sports world too, we find this phenomenon of pressure and stress, the causes are diverse.

A hectic life filled with various activities and obligations often leads to enormous pressure, a professional life sometimes boring or nonexistent, our dependence, new means of communication (smartphones, internet, emails) do not always encourage relaxation.

Many experts urge you to reorganize your personal and professional life, when stress is too important or difficult to live with. But we know that this is not so simple everyday.

Some experts have been studying for years how to effectively manage stress and its effects by advocating micronutrients.

They find today, a significant increase in patients developing stress. Patients complain of ailments such as increased state of agitation, persistent sleep disorders and impaired concentration.

These patients are people who are under a lot of pressure in their professional life, like managers or even homemakers.

They also find that athletes are affected by the pressure of stress. Indeed, stress is a hindrance to performance.

That's why they focus on taking dietary supplements to combat stress. For several years, we have obtained very good results with the help of micronutrients.

Imagine our body, and that each cell of it is like a central one. Thus, this plant produces energy, but during the production of energy, toxins are released and these toxins are called free radicals.

Normally, these free radicals can be very well neutralized, but when the machines are running at full speed constantly, the amount of free radicals released becomes so great that the body is unable to neutralize them alone and that's when that stress invades us and decreases or limits our performance.

What can we do to combat these negative effects?

We can provide our body with sufficient micronutrients, such as vitamin E, selenium, as well as very active plant elements such as chlorophyll, green tea and especially resveratrol.

Resveratrol is actually one of the strongest antioxidants. Per unit of time, it can trap a large amount of free radicals and thus effectively reduce stress.

It is good to capture free radicals, but we need more micronutrients to boost energy supply. There may be mentioned vitamins b, choline, L-carnitine, iron, as well as coenzyme Q10 which are particularly important.

The Q10, a major supplier of energy because it directly supports the mitochondria, our plant. Nutrients such as iron, among others, help to ensure the transport of oxygen.

With regard to the mind and in order to increase our memory capacity and our psyche, we need B vitamins and cholines which are important for supplying our nerve cells with sugar.

And if you regularly take an optimal mix from these micronutrients, you will feel better in your body, but also better in your head. We will be in better shape, we will have a greater concentration capacity and we will feel less stressed.

CHAPTER 6

FINANCIAL STRESS

Many of us seek some financial freedom, but not only the environment we are in does not support us, but the choices we make on a daily basis only worsen our case.

Before reaching financial freedom, we must first admit that the bonds that constrain us so that we can get rid of them, when we prefer to use our money in our own way as we see fit.

Currently in the Western world, when we do not pay off our debts, we do not go to jail physically. However annually, a large amount of people are ruined by annoyances, by the constraints produced by the accumulation of debts.

Financial stress occurs when there is a buildup of debt or when our weakness in our assets causes us a lot of problems or when we make a precarious use.

Financial stress is at the same time a behavior and a situation or attitude that is the effect caused by the excessive use of our means.

It is essential to know that no one is out of reach of financial stress. The fortunate, because usually prosperity brings anxiety, the uncertainty of dispossessing what one has. As the needy, because the insufficiency also causes anguish, the concern for the future.

Financial stress or financial dependence is a behavior and condition that depends on our choice to administer our money as we see fit.

What are the signs and symptoms of financial stress?

The main sign of financial stress is our debts. We suffer from anxiety, dissatisfaction and grief when we are in debt or cannot repay even a simple bill.

Normally, we get into debt when we spend beyond what we cash. And one of the reasons that drive us to do this is a lack of foresight, because good planning would allow us to see and guard against certain unhealthy financial situations.

We go into debt when we spend beyond what we can afford and the only way to spend what we do not have is when we borrow. It is therefore not surprising that the loan is a parameter that contributes to financial stress.

Another symptom of financial stress is fear, if you feel too dominated by the worry of losing your money or the fear of losing your job, losing your home or something else.

The desire to be rich suddenly is present. It is in this reason that each year a large number of individuals are absorbed by all types of fraud, in their pursuit to become rich too fast. This state of mind leads us to indulge ourselves sometimes abusively and to consider others unfairly.

To be fraudulent is not only to cheat, but it is also not to be completely honest with others. A person, who has an ability to lie or not to be completely loyal when it comes to his finances, already displays a symptom of financial stress.

Unfortunately, many people are convinced that you cannot prosper and be loyal at the same time. It's also one of the many mystifications that society wants us to do.

If you are not faithful in the little things, you will not be faithful in the big things.

The desire is also a symptom of financial stress. You always feel insatiable about what you own, you want more and more, you acquire things without regard to their role, you want tirelessly to have the most recent model, you buy without thinking.

Want to hold something that belongs to someone else; want everything we see at the store, want everything we are shown through the media, covetousness.

What are the causes of financial stress?

Generally, the causes of financial stress come together around the following four factors:

1) The lack of money
2) Unnecessary expenses
3) The fortune
4) The ignorance

What are the solutions to financial stress?

a- Avoid consumer credit, because it is the main source of debt and preferably you will stop borrowing, the faster you will be relieved of your debts.
b- Prepare a budget. The budget helps you spend your money in a calculated and strategic way. It simplifies your daily decisions and helps you make better use of your financial resources. If you owe a

lot, your budget will be more unpleasant during the time of debt repayment.

c- Set up a payment program. Call your creditors to renegotiate your loan.

d- To put an end to the domination of materialism by giving to the needy.

CHAPTER 7

MONEY

The first assumption about the appearance of money is that it was designed to simplify trade. Of course, it was not always certain to exchange a cow for a wheat field. Not very effective and a little embarrassing, the coins certainly made things easier.

It can thus be said that money has two roles with this hypothesis. Its main role is to help estimate a product, a service. A value is determined for a product, and this value is interpreted as money.

Its second function is to facilitate exchanges. In the modern world, we do not trade cows for harvests anymore, but our time and our knowledge. Most of the time, you will receive compensation in exchange for the time you spend putting your knowledge to the service of your hirer or your clients.

Easy money does not exist. Smart money exists. Money dominates our society, it's a reality. The man needs the money to trade and buy. Money is a very attractive design and if there is one thing I understood, it is that money can be an occasion of misfortune as well as of well-being.

Money is not bad; it's the love of money that is bad. It is necessary to consider the money in a mathematical way without carrying of the emotional one (it is that which makes it possible to control the money).

Money in itself has no value, what matters is what we make of it.

Money makes it possible to feed oneself, to lodge, to go out, to travel, to clothe oneself, to educate oneself, to heal oneself. And yet, with only the money, you can go beyond many other great things while on earth, as well as make friends, seduce a person, have confidence in oneself, be creative, increase one's performances (mental or physical), develop one's spirituality, appreciate a landscape, etc.

It is these things that will fill you up and make you blossom.

Finally, we can say that money is an instrument that allows us to express thanks.

Where does the money come from?

There are two limitations to the understanding of the current financial system:

Money is an untouchable theme that is not currently questioned.

Money is not taught at school or later. This is a generally obscure idea for the majority of people who have not attended training in economics. Consequently, one does not question what one does not apprehend.

Few people know that it is no longer the public administration that produces most of the money (the national bank or the federal agency still creates the currency but not the electronic money).

Moreover, what few people know is that the banks produce the money they lend, they do not have it. Other types of money are possible and can boost the economy but in particular increase the purchasing power of the population.

Initially, barter only allowed trade. Also now in Africa barter is of great importance both at the individual level and between companies. The difficulty of bartering: it is very restrictive because it is necessary to identify the individual who is interested in exchanging what you have to offer and who more precisely is what you are looking for.

Throughout history and all over the world all kinds of things are used as currency, such as pearls, cocoa beans, seashells, salt, amber, ivory, stones, feathers, tobacco, etc. Some things are adopted as money because they are portable, others because they have decorative value and still others because they can be consumed. All are recognized as an acceptable means of exchange or as a means of settling their debts.

Thus is born the ancestor of money that allows the exchange between people using a "value" accepted and recognized as such by a community. "Your calf is worth 100 shells and with these 100 shells you can buy eggs, a plow and chickens for your sister's wedding".

Thus is born this fantastic but natural invention that is money, VECTOR EXCHANGE between men. It is at the base of the structure of societies and without it no civilization could emerge.

In Mesopotamia, the first cuneiform writings, on clay tablets, were accounting entries. A system of administrative management of debts and debts has developed. It was based on the comparison of the value of traded products with "standard values" known to all (given amount of cereals, gold, or silver).

In Egypt and Mesopotamia, scriptural money existed long before fiduciary money (several thousand years). But with the intensification and diversification of trade, this has necessitated a bloated administration and consequently a much too heavy taxation.

It was therefore necessary to simplify: find a way to settle a debt by a simple and reliable means: the "fiduciary" currency.

Etymological parenthesis: "credit" comes from the Latin credere = to believe, to trust; "Debit" comes from the Latin debitus = what is due, debt; in the same vein, "fiduciary" comes from the Latin fiducia, ae = trust.

A stallion has emerged in every human group: shells, small works of art, minerals or small ingots of more or less precious metal or goods of common use, such as salt that was used to pay the Roman legionnaires (it is the origin of the word salary). Symbolic objects were also used, such as the "coin-axes" of the late Bronze Age discovered in Britain.

In the fourteenth century, among the Aztecs, the cocoa bean was a means of exchange recognized throughout Mesoamerica. A slave is then worth 100 beans, the favors of a courtesan: 80 beans and a rabbit: 10 beans. Alms to a beggar amount to 3 or 4 beans.

In fact, the value of the currency is not equal to the market value of the beans.

In some countries, it was not until the twentieth century to see the disappearance of these primitive forms of money. This was particularly the case of shackles (slave rings) or shells in parts of Africa. Kauri shells (or cowries) were used in China 5th century AD. In India, then throughout the Pacific. It is found in the early fourteenth century Maldives, where Arab traders have exported to the east coast of Africa.

They then transit through Sudan to Guinea, then to Mauritania and to the Berbers of the Atlas. Until the nineteenth century, kauri values spread primarily in East Africa, particularly in Zanzibar and Ethiopia.

After 1870, colonial governments sought to ban kauris as currency. But men were used to it and always used it as "small change". It was not until 1955 that kauri values became almost completely out of order.

In ancient Greece the currency spread rapidly from the 8th century BC. According to Herodotus the Lydians (now Turkey) are the first to design silver and gold coins. The use of this kind of room spreads throughout Greece and each city begins to hit its own pieces.

In Greece, mainly in silver, the pieces are of a strictly identical weight. Then bronze allows daily exchanges of low values. Metallic money is a valuable standard: metals are divisible by weight. It is therefore possible to match the value of parts to their weight, which facilitates trade and commerce.

Alexander the Great (-356 BC) reserves the right to coin money. He quickly created a unique imperial currency. The new drachma is spreading everywhere. (The "electrum" kind of natural white gold was indeed rejected by the rivers that crossed at Sardinian capital of Lydia.Cresus (-550 BC) would have been the first to strike gold coins and pure silver The important element was the affixing of a mark or hallmark by an institution guaranteeing the exchange value of the coin As early as -450 BC, we find the use of money in Marseilles.

Previously in China were minted coins in the form of miniature tools (knives, spades, ..). It was not until the third century BC that Emperor Shi Huangdi struck round coins pierced with a square hole in the middle.

It was in Rome, in the third century before Christ, that a first monetary workshop began. It was installed on the Capitol, near the temple of Junon "Moneta". At other times, the geese guarded near the temple had warned the Romans of a night attack of the Gauls, which had earned the goddess Junon the qualifier of Moneta (warner), a term from which are derived the words currency, moneda, money ...

The first Roman metal coins (aes or as) were small bronze ingots adorned with an ox. They were replaced by sesterces. The denier (denarius or piece of ten), struck in silver, was the first coin to bear a value inscribed in the form of an X, for 10 aces.

Then, at the beginning of our era, Auguste reorganized the monetary system on the principle of trimetallism. The aureus weighs about 8 g of gold, its parity with the silver denier is fixed at 1 / 25th. The denier itself equals 4 sesterces of bronze.

With the development of the Empire, the Roman monetary system is widely needed. Coinages of exchange, the coins also become instruments of propaganda to the glory of the emperor. The political instability and decadence of the Empire are accompanied by a deterioration of the currency.

Similarly, the gradual scarcity of money leads to a break in parities and a loss of confidence in the respective value of coins.

To stop this movement, Constantine I, at the same time that he reorganized the Empire, imposes monometallism and puts into circulation a new gold coin designed to last and serve as a reference: solidus (solid, in

Latin). The first solidus are struck at Trier, in the Rhineland, in the year 310.

After the fall of the Western Roman Empire, the use of this currency continues for a long time in Byzantium. In the West, even though its circulation is shrinking more rapidly, it continues to play a role as a unit of account for nearly a millennium. Francised in soil or sou, the term has passed through the centuries; he also gave "pay" and "soldier".

The gold came mainly from the Mediterranean, especially the coins of the Byzantine Empire, the nomisma, and then the besant. But around 650, the economic and monetary geography was changed to the benefit of the North, from which came the "sceattas", Anglo-Saxon and Frisian silver coins (current Netherlands).

In addition, gold is becoming scarce and more expensive after the fall of Byzantine Africa and the capture of Carthage.

Around 675, in Gaul, the gold sou is completed, and then replaced by a piece of silver, the denier, the name of the ancient Roman money money. Twelve deniers make a penny. The pieces are produced everywhere and have many aspects.

In 692, Caliph Abd al-Malik of Damascus introduced the Golden Dinar into the Muslim world. It will become the reference currency throughout the Mediterranean and beyond for centuries.

The Byzantine and Arab monetary reforms, the success of the Anglo-Frisian currencies, the exploitation of new silver deposits and internal political circumstances perpetuate the adoption of the silver standard under the aegis of the Carolingians. Charlemagne, lacking a sufficient supply of gold, resigned himself to putting into circulation new money of reference, the silver money (from 1.36 g to 1.80 g of silver).

By prescribing to cut 240 deniers in a pound of silver, Charlemagne lays the foundations of a monetary and accounting system that will persist, in France until the Revolution: 1 pound = 20 sous or 240 deniers, and a sou = 12 deniers and in the United Kingdom until 1971. In addition, is struck a division of the denarius, the silver obole, which corresponds to its half.

In the great period of economic expansion of the middle Ages, the gold coins also reappeared. The first is the florin of Florence in 1252, followed by the ducat of Venice. Saint Louis creates the "tournaments" of silver and the shield, worth 10 under tournaments.

The first international currency of modern times has been struck in Austria. In 1750, in order to reconnect with the success of the Reichsthaler of Emperor Ferdinand I (1559), the Empress Maria Theresa of Habsburg had a golden thaler engraved with her effigy. The Maria Theresien Thaler (MTT) will soon become a popular international currency in the Spanish and English colonies of America, and to East Africa. After the death of the Sovereign, in 1780, she will continue to be struck with the date of 1780.

The word dollar is itself a distortion of the word thaler, the currency of Marie-Thérèse having been the first used by the planters of North America.

While money already represents a certain amount of goods, which could not be manipulated so easily, the next step is the establishment of a second-rate currency, which itself represents a large amount of metallic money left in safe deposit.

Thus appears the paper money (the banknote, known in China since the eighth century), which originally represents only a debt payable on sight in the form of metal or other goods.

The bill of exchange, invented by Italian merchants, is one of the first ways of replacing paper with metal.

In China, the first bank notes were already circulating during the Tang Dynasty (618-907). The official coin consisted of very heavy iron pieces of little value. Instead of transporting these cumbersome pieces with them, they were deposited with merchants against delivery of a bill of exchange, which soon replaced the coins as a means of payment.

The Chinese called this new currency "the flying currency" because it was very light and could easily be used in all circumstances.

In the early 11th century, Chinese traders united to issue fixed-value banknotes, the Jiao Zi, printed on wooden boards with vermilion and black inks. Each ticket was unique and provided with a unique number to prevent counterfeiting.

But the introduction of the first bills raised many problems, because the traders sometimes printed more than they had coins on their reserves. The Song Dynasty was finally forced to control the issuance of Jiao Zi notes.

In the year 1168, a paper mill, owned by the government, began to make the paper on which the notes were printed from the gray bark of the mulberry tree.

In the thirteenth century, mulberry bark was replaced by silk. When Marco Polo returned from his trip to China and talked about the paper money of the Chinese, the Europeans would not believe it: they could not imagine a currency without "material" value.

Over the centuries, the decoration of banknotes became more and more sophisticated. The Chinese bank note is not only provided with a very ornate border, it also carries its value in strings of coins.

Despite many counterfeits, which were punishable by the death penalty, the paper money remained a payment instrument appreciated by the Chinese. The rulers of the Ming Dynasty (1368-1644) even banned metal coin for a hundred years.

Skeptical, Europeans considered paper money, until an advanced period, as an exotic curiosity.

Its introduction in Sweden in the seventeenth century is not enough to improve its reputation because it led to inflation and scandal. In Germany, every attempt to introduce paper money raised hurricanes of indignation.

When, in 1661, Sweden experienced its first shortage of silver, and because of the devaluation of the copper coin, the economy was ravaged by inflation, the Dutchman Johann Palmstruck was welcomed as the savior of the nation in distress.

He proposed to introduce bills of exchange and founded the first Swedish bank (Stockholm Bank) which issued the first "certificates" on July 16, 1661.

The denominations were numbered by hand and bore the signatures of the bank's employees. This did not prevent them from being often imitated and the bank was forced to introduce three new security marks: a watermark paper, eleven different stamps and complicated ornaments on the edges.

In 1745, Sweden adopted banknotes as official currency. Other European countries were soon persuaded by paper money, which gained its proper place in the monetary system.

Originally from Venice, Marco Polo, who lived at the court of the Chinese ruler Kublai Khan at the end of the 13th century, reports: "All these pieces of paper are printed with the same seriousness and solemnity as if it were hitting pure gold or silver, each copy must be signed and stamped by many officials, year after year, the Khan has printed paper money in an amount so impressive that it probably has to match the value of all the treasures of this earth ".

In 1661, the banker Johann Palmstruck introduced the bank note in Europe. When silver-money ran out in Sweden, he printed tickets. However, Palmstruck did not resist the temptation to put more notes into circulation than his bank could repay. This led to bankruptcy in 1668. She was monopolized by the state and Palmstruck was sentenced to death. But, thanks to the intervention of the king, he was saved.

We can distinguish several stages in the historical evolution that led from the metallic money to the fiduciary money that we know today:

1) Bimetallism (until the 19th century): all currencies are defined both in relation to gold and in relation to silver (metal). Each State, depending on its availability of metal, preferentially uses one or the other metal, and uses the other as an adjunct. In particular, gold and silver coins, by their intrinsic value, circulate frequently outside their country of origin.

   Mining discoveries and financial developments in a largely globalized economy at the time caused the proportions of the two metals to fluctuate, and the development of paper money and credit made it possible to limit the need for metal, and to eliminate silver-metal as stallion.

2) The "classic" gold standard (until 1914): all currencies are defined in relation to gold. Paper money is a substitute for gold (an ounce of gold equals 20 dollars, 4 British pounds, etc.). The conversion rates of each currency into gold, and therefore between them, are fixed. This ensures the stability of the currency and prevents artificially induced inflation by an increase in the money supply (a process that states will constantly use thereafter).

   In 1865, the Latin Monetary Union was created, a monetary agreement between Belgium, France, Italy and Switzerland, to which Greece adhered in

1868. This convention remained in force, with several adjustments, until 1st module, title, weight) which thus had a cross-border circulation. Its purpose was to harmonize the currencies of these countries.

3) The gold exchange standard (1914-1971): this is a mixed system whereby some countries want to retain the benefits of the gold standard, while others want to keep the latitude (via the "Printing press") to have variable exchange rates. This system will become obsolete in a few decades:

World War I: Due to the cost of war all European currencies are heavily devalued in relation to gold.

1922: Genoa conference. A new monetary order is in place where only the United States retains the classic gold standard. The dollar is based on gold, the British pound on the dollar and other European currencies on the British pound.

1931: the United Kingdom, led to increase its money supply, abandons the gold-exchange system.

1934: the dollar is defined as 1/35 of an ounce of gold. US citizens do not have the right to own gold.

1944: Bretton Woods's agreements: the monetary system is based on the dollar, the only currency still anchored in gold.

1971: under Nixon, the United States, no longer able to keep the price of gold at $ 35 an ounce or avoid a devaluation of the dollar, abandons the gold standard.

4) The floating exchange rate (from March 1973): after the abandonment of the Bretton Woods agreements, the currencies vary freely, depending on supply and demand, and therefore in principle according to the amount of credit issued by each country (a lax monetary policy is "punished" by a decline in the value of the local currency relative to other currencies).

There is no longer any metallic counterpart to the currency issued, only debt.

Summary of different types of currencies

a- The metal currency

Metal money is also a savings tool: precious metals can be kept in a safe, under a mattress, in a hiding place without losing much value, they can even take some. They can be reshaped to beat other currencies so they never lose their intrinsic value.

The obstacle of metallic money is that it is attached to the quantity of precious metal available.

b- Fiduciary money

Fiduciary money collects bank notes spread by the central bank and coins distributed by the Treasury. The concept of "fiduciary money" refers to the origin of bank notes. The notes had strength only if the central bank had its gold counterpart. Fiduciary money is a currency created on the confidence granted to the economy of a country. Currently, a central bank of a country can issue notes without having the gold counterpart.

The value of a currency is fixed by the confidence that one grants to it and which one grants to the country. The first banknotes are born in Sweden around 1660 AD. Fiduciary money is the whole currency issued by a state in the form of coin or banknote, while these coins and notes indicate a value transcending their real value.

c- Scriptural money

The scriptural money is not materialized by a material tool such as coins or banknotes. The scriptural money is concretized by an accounting entry on a check or a bank account. The scriptural money is the one that realizes on the bank accounts and moves thanks to the flows (movements, exchanges) monetary.

This currency is imperceptible but it is achieved by bank entries, at the bottom of a bank statement, on a check to cash, in the books of accounts of the bank.

It is also realized through bank cards, electronic wallet cards; the scriptural money apprehends:

- The checks

The check is a writing by which the holder of a deposit account asks his bank to pay money to another person. The check is valid for 1 year plus 8 days. Checks are not payable in cash, to receive the amount you need an account.

- Transfers

This transaction allows a person to transfer money from one account to another account.

- Telepayments

It is all means of remote payment from the phone or the Internet.

- Mandates

The money order is a means of payment managed by Post; it allows sending a sum of money to another person.

- The cards

There are different types of cards. They are issued by banking institutions or commercial networks. They can withdraw money, shop at a merchant or receive credit.

Electronic wallet cards. They make it possible to make purchases of small amounts at the merchants and on certain automata. They are recharged on terminals or directly at the merchants.

Payment cards. These are bank cards or cards like Visa-Eurocard-Mastercard credit cards. They can be national or international.

CHAPTER 8

LOVE

Love is a secret for those who experience it, an enigma for those who observe it. We notice, but we do not apprehend.

What attaches us to the other is indefinable. To really love is to have someone else in his life, not only for his appearance, nor for what he characterizes, but for his mystery.

This mystery that we do not know how to challenge, and who will join ours.

Well, love is the confrontation of two lesions, two fissures, and the distribution with someone of what we absolutely miss and that we will not be able to express.

True love is not a business deal; it's an aggressive feeling that puts both employees at risk.

To love is to want the other. Love can be referred to as intense emotion that drives the individual who feels it to pursue an approach with the loved one.

Obviously, the intensity varies according to each one that is to say weak, strong or obsessional, and thus difficult to control.

The original love is revealed by various indications that do not deceive, such as pulsations, the throat that is knotted, the hands that are moist, or also a continuous happiness that clogs us in the spirit or the sight of this to be desired.

In other words, it is possible to realize the difference between love and friendship.

To be able to please, you must have had the charm. To feel seduced, we need attention that personalizes, that makes us believe that we are extraordinary.

Seduction takes only on the reciprocal feeling, which needs to show a part of ourselves which most of us do not even have a fixed idea. It is not a question of divulging our deficiencies, but of revealing our elegance.

Without this influx of emotions, one can provoke affection, cause ecstasy also, or attachment, the desire to be a friend, however there could be no childbirth of the amorous aspect.

Seduction is hiding in our precedent. Everyone can seduce when we expose the part of one that is not very far from our authenticity, close to this famous enigma.

Creating a sensation is actually engaging. In relationships between couples in general, there must be a balance between giving and taking.

And when you become aware of the orders of love and intuition, you can make soul movements that decrease the tension of the bonds.

Relationships are a clear example where you have to take into account, give and take as a law of relations, because these are two people who are at the same level, where the sacred order means that both are in equal conditions and any lack must be compensated for maintaining the balance.

While relationships between couples are one of the greatest challenges, they can also become the fusion of two male and female forces, integrated into unity for the transformation of humanity.

For that, it is essential to establish relations of equality, between giving and taking, so that this balance can go from one side to the other and where for moments you can enjoy the ecstasy in a perfect balance because, as in life itself, existence tends to go rhythmically in search of its balance between chaos and creation.

For couples it is essential that no member of her receives more than necessary because the message that is transmitted is (I'm the little one, take care of me), which on the one hand can make you want to find someone one with whom you can be in equal relationships or the weight will be so great that it will only be removed leaving the relationship.

On the other hand, the one who continues to give more can also play the father or the mother, that is to say, play the big one, you can easily see when a member of the couple speaks and says (is that I have to take care of my partner, very immature).

This kind of relationship has the days counted for it to end.

In couple relationships, compensation is needed, the same system calls for balance, for example if a person cannot give children in a relationship, she has one (type of debt) with the other and the both must be aware of the price paid and indemnify him.

Relationships that last over time are those where there is a more or less permanent balance, and does not mean that you have to give more in a relationship, is to give in the right measure and constantly compensate, if one of the members of the relationship is wrong, the other has the responsibility to compensate this debt by something of less value and not to be put in the place of the victim, not to do justice, to play the good but to have behavior (passive, aggressive) that will generate tension in the relationship.

For the good of the relationship, it is essential that each member take the responsibility to take what is right and give the right, if not more, because both establish this sacred bond that can unite them for life, if they respect the balance that their own system drives them to follow consciously or unconsciously.

The perfect couple does not exist. The perfect man or woman exists only in our imagination.

The inequalities of each are neither an element of anxiety nor an element of risk. They feed us even.

Every love encounter always brings tangle, both external and internal. Sensations, troubles, manners.

Sex is good for health, naturally because the happiness of making love makes you happy, and the state of well-being is good for the immune system.

The physical pleasure, source of energy, helps a better hormonal stability.

The bursting of endorphins in the brain at the moment of orgasm produces this perception of euphoria, then of happiness, tranquility, reduction of stress and anxiety and recuperative sleep.

In a happy marriage, there are three kinds of love. It will be useful if we consider them as three parts of a pyramid.

First, the base of the pyramid is a special type of love that we call "agape". The central part of the pyramid is the love of friendship and the upper part is physical or sexual love. Consider these three kinds of love. Let's start with love "agape".

Agape love is the love that gives and sacrifices for what is best for the other person. Agape love has two main characteristics: it is not selfish (it seeks what is best for the person it loves) and it is a love of commitment (continue to love whatever happens).

Agape love is not just a beautiful feeling; it's a final decision of the will.

One of the amazing things about love agape is this, when you decide to love a person without selfishness and to behave with that person with love, over time you will have the feeling of love.

Remember, you do not have to wait until you feel love for other members of your family. You can decide to love them and begin to behave selflessly with them. It is an excellent training for the wedding.

Any boy or girl can behave affectionately with the person with whom he is planning to marry.

It suits him to do it. But once they are married and the routine of daily life is established, their basic nature will be expressed.

If they are selfish in their current family situation, they will be selfish in their marriage.

One of the biggest mistakes young people make is getting married quickly because they cannot live at home.

But until you learn to live at home, accepting and loving other members of your family, you are not really ready for marriage.

Before considering marriage, you must be sure that you have agape love for that special person and that he or she also has that kind of love for you.

A happy marriage is not a marriage between two "perfect" people who know each other and get married. There are no "perfect" people!

A happy marriage is a marriage between two imperfect people who love each other with a committed love that is not selfish. Agape love is not blind: see the faults of the other, but cover them with love.

When you really love someone, you do not try to change it. You accept it and love it as it is. Agape love says, "I love you, whatever happens, and I will always love you."

You can see why this kind of love is essential for a happy and successful marriage.

Agape love is not just for marriage. We must develop agape love for all people.

The love of friendship. It is the love and tender affection we have for good friends, the people we love to be with. We must have this kind of love for people of our sex, as well as for the opposite sex.

We must develop agape love without selfishness for all, but not everyone can be a close friend. The illustration of the pyramid shows how the objects of our affection begin to diminish when we reach the level of love of friendship.

To have a happy marriage, you must have the love of friendship for your spouse so that they can enjoy being together, talking and sharing things with each other.

A marriage without tender affection between husband and wife will not be satisfactory even if there is a lot of passion in the bedroom.

Physical or sexual love this is the most special and intimate love shared by a husband and his wife.

We must have sexual love with one person - with whom we are married. The pyramid illustrates how our affection is reduced to one person when it reaches the level of sexual love.

In the beginning, God created a man and a woman. I was committed to each other for life. It is God's conception of marriage and sexual love: a man and a woman engaged in life.

God has conceived of sex as a means of reproducing children as a source of pleasure. Through sex, a husband and wife can fully express their love for each other. It is one of the greatest privileges and blessings of marriage.

This command prohibits any sexual impurity. Adultery is a sexual relationship between a married person and someone other than their spouse. Fornication is a sexual relationship between a man and a woman who is not married.

But as beautiful as sexual love may be, it can never be the foundation of a successful marriage.

Many couples try to build their marriage on the basis of physical or sexual love. The wedding may last for a while, but when the storms of life come, your marriage will fail.

The couple will discover too late that they cannot build a happy and successful marriage with sexual love as a foundation.

However, it is very important that these three types of love come together in the right order.

First of all, for a happy and successful marriage, you must have love agape (love that is not selfish and who wants the best for the other person).

Then you need the love of friendship (that love that allows husband and wife to love being together). Finally, in a happy marriage, there is a sexual love that satisfies.

Unfortunately, many young people focus on physical or sexual love. They throw themselves into physical intimacy without knowing if they have agape love and friendship for each other. It may sound more exciting, but it's like trying to build a pyramid! It will not work.

The desire to have sex is something that God has created in us. It's not dirty or bad.

Sexual desire was the idea of God (not ours). He created in us those hormones that make the opposite sex attractive to us. Sexual relations, as God designed them, are beautiful.

The sexual impulse can be compared to hunger. It is not a sin to be hungry, but it is a sin to steal food to satisfy our hunger. In the same way, the sexual impulse in itself is not a sin, but it is a sin if we satisfy that desire in the wrong way.

The sexual impulse as God planned it. God has created all living things that can reproduce. Animals have a powerful sexual impulse that unites the male and the female for sexual intercourse.

However, in the case of animals, libido is in certain seasons. The female receives the male only during the time she is in heat. The rest of the time she has no interest in sex. Apparently, in the case of animals, God designed the sexual drive solely for the purpose of reproduction.

With humans, it's different. God has given us sexual desire as well as means of reproduction as a means by which husband and wife can more fully express their love for each other.

In marriage, the strong sexual desire that arises when the husband and wife are stimulated can be legitimately satisfied by sexual intercourse.

But these same strong desires and passions can be stimulated outside marriage.

However, in this case, there is no legitimate solution for these stimulated desires. Stopping without consuming sex produces frustration, and doing the act is fornication (one of the most harmful sins a young person can commit).

We can compare sexual desire with a steam boiler. When a fire is activated in the boiler, the water inside becomes steam. This steam is under enormous pressure, but it is equipped with an appropriate exhaust.

Steam is used to drive a turbine that produces electricity. However, if you light a fire in a boiler that does not have a safe exhaust for steam, the boiler will explode.

A love relationship is a relationship between a boy and a girl, in which everyone agrees not to go out with another person. Almost everyone wants to have someone to talk to (with whom to share their joys and problems).

Being a couple is not only nice, it has real benefits.

Being in a relationship will help you develop socially. Being with someone of the opposite sex at the beginning will be uncomfortable, but it will help you learn to feel comfortable with someone of the opposite sex.

Being in a relationship will help you develop your personality. You will learn how to deal with difficult situations and how to grow and mature in your relationships with others.

Being in a relationship will help you choose your spouse. Almost all young people want to get married one day. It is also a way to meet your possible marriage partner. This is valuable because it helps you decide what kind of person you want to marry.

There is also a danger in the relationship. The danger is that you are doing something that could seriously affect your chances of future happiness and a successful marriage.

It's easy for young people to think (I have my life in front of me; the decisions I make today will not change anything).

To marry someone with the hope of changing him would be more or less like starting a plane without a parachute. The chances of having a safe and healthy landing are almost equal in both cases.

As dangerous as it is, many girls are willing to compromise their future happiness by marrying a young man in the hope of changing him.

A girl can say (I know that my boyfriend drinks a lot, and he likes to flirt with other girls, but I think that will change after our wedding).

These thoughts are vain desires that are very bad. It does not change the fundamental nature of a person when she gets married. If there are problems before marriage, they will probably get worse later.

If your love is real, you will be interested in the total personality of the person you love. There is no doubt, there is an exciting element in physical attraction, but this is just one of the many things about the person who attracts you.

If it's true love, you will be attracted to many or almost all of the qualities of the other person. Each of us has endless characteristics, attitudes and opinions. How many did you observe in the other person? How much do you attract?

This is important because after the initial emotion of being married is over, you will need to have a lot in common for your marriage to continue to have vitality.

True love always begins slowly. It cannot be otherwise. You need to know someone before you can really love them, and it takes a lot of time to really meet someone.

A long parade is much better than a short one. A year is better than six months and two years are better than one.

Yes, the statistics are very clear on this subject. But most young people do not even wait a year. Many who throw themselves into marriage learn from sad experience that they would have listened to the saying that: Before you get married, looks what you are doing. If you make the mistake of rushing for marriage, you will have plenty of time later to regret not looking at what you have done.

In true love, your feelings are probably warm and tender instead of hot or cold, and more likely to be continuous. True love develops slowly, but the roots become deep.

If your love is real, the person you love will shine on your best qualities and make you want to be a better person.

A young man who was really in love said: (I love my girlfriend, not only because she is wonderful, but because she encourages me to be the person I should be).

In true love, your loved one is the most important person in the world for you, but your relationships with family and friends also continue to be important.

In true love, it is likely that your parents and most of your friends approve of the relationship.

In true love, the absence makes your heart fall more and more in love with the loved one. True love can survive the test of time and distance. And he will survive.

True love has its roots in the total personality of the other person, not just in his physical appearance. The time they spent together meant that their personalities met.

When they separate, part of you seems to be missing. No other person, as attractive as it is, can fill the void in your heart.

When they are separated, maybe you worry a little, in addition to feeling sad. But if you're loved one can be happier with another person, it's better that you find out now and not after the wedding. So, if the court ends, accept it and do not worry. If the relationship is a whim and does not survive, it's best to find out before it's too late.

In true love, there will be arguments, but true love will always survive the trials and over time they will be less frequent and less severe.

Each couple must learn to deal with conflicts. It is better to discuss differences frankly than to allow them to grow underground.

This key may not seem to be very important during the relationship, but it has a great importance in the marriage.

In a marriage based on a whim, the husband and wife may appreciate more about developing their separate interests than doing things together. The husband may prefer "hanging out with friends" rather than staying at home with his family. Or a woman might have more interest in their social contacts than in their home obligations.

In a marriage where true love exists, husband and wife enjoy doing things together. They usually say, "I do not want to go if you cannot go with me."

In true love, you love the person for what they are (not because they make you feel important).

True love is not selfish, it is a committed love. You want to do everything you can to bring happiness to the other person. Your general attitude is to give the relationship and not take all the benefits you can.

Some people make the decision not to marry, and this is probably an acceptable decision, but most people decide to get married.

Getting married is easy. But having a happy and successful marriage is not easy. This is not a good luck.

There are specific things you can do to dramatically improve your chances of a happy marriage.

CHAPTER 9

FRIENDSHIP

Friendship is a shared affection, a mark of bilateral affection between two individuals who do not belong to the same family.

The relationship is close to the relationship, with the exception of exclusivity and sexual affinity. Friendship is often built on collective attachments and similar abilities.

Friends usually meet at their workplace or during their sporting or cultural activities.

Friendship has five essential rules: sincerity, secrecy, recognition, loyalty and truthfulness.

A friend, also someone else and someone with confidence, who creates alchemy, is based on an approach that is sometimes difficult to decipher.

We cannot ask his friends to convert. If you admire them, you support them with their awkwardness.

We are allowed to agree with whom we will link a friendship relationship. If clumsiness suffocates you too much, it is essential to interrupt this relationship.

Try to be a very good friend you can rely on at any time. Attempt to be there when we need you. To be a good friend is to be there in moments of joy, but especially in bad times.

The basis of a good friendship is the common values. In other words, good friends share moral, spiritual and ethical convictions.

The next factor, compatibility, is less important.

And, often, having the same interests is the least important thing.

After all, it is possible to have friends with hobbies and talents different from those of one.

Be careful with friendships that are based exclusively on common interests. If they do not share your values, the relationship will surely be fragile and could even get you into trouble.

The five (5) characteristics of a true friend:

1) Genuinely cares for you

It does not appear only when you need it or when you have nothing better to do. That is why he is aware of what is happening to you and does not wait for you to seek him out to be present.

He is interested in knowing you and will be the first to arrive when you are going through a serious problem.

The anxiety he feels for you is disinterested. He just loves you and wants you to be healed.

Do not "die" if something bad happens to you, or if you have the emotional intensity of other relationships, but you still have the certainty that it is there.

2) *He wants to understand you, he does not judge you*

Friendship implies mutual acceptance. A true friend does not want to change you, or criticize you or challenge your life.

He knows you have mistaken, but he does not want to report them. And if that's the case, it's probably in the intention that you suffer less and you do not become someone else.

A true friend is open to understanding. If you tell him about your problems, he will try to understand your position and not point out your mistakes.

For this reason, with this person, you feel comfortable to be yourself, to show yourself as you are.

A friend is a person with whom you can think aloud.

3) *Alleviate difficult situations*

A true friend knows that he is not your mother, nor your confessor, nor your psychologist. That's why, instead of preaching or giving a pulpit to live well, share the difficult moments with you in a spontaneous and simple way.

If you know you're fried, invite them to eat ice cream or take a walk in the park. If you know that you are going through an unpleasant situation, you will take the drama and the joke with you to make the matter less serious.

If you know that you are suffering, you will be at your side in a serene and non-invasive way.

4) *He knows how to listen to you*

If something distinguishes true friendship, it is this listening ability, which goes well beyond silence while another speaks. True listening is respectful and warm. He is also attentive to the words of the other and helps him to listen to himself.

To know how to listen does not interfere with what the other person says, if it is not necessary. It is accepting what the other expresses, without gestures or attitudes of disapproval.

Listening is about silently accompanying someone, while giving shape to their ideas and feelings through words.

5) *He is sincere and forgets easy*

Great friends do not pretend, or what they think of you, or how they feel about you.

The charm of friendship is precisely that people involved trust and knows what to expect from each other.

There is no place for false courtesy, or for hypocrisy, among true friends.

In other types of relationships, an aversion or a fight can get bigger. But in friendship, no. True friendship easily forgets these conflicts and turns the page without problems.

Of course, there are limits, but in friendship, daily disagreements make little sense.

True friendship is built between two. More than considering whether your friends meet all of these requirements, we invite you to do the exercise of evaluating how good you are a friend.

For sure, who knows how to be a friend finds real friends.

In a way, a true friend is a shoulder on which to pity who does not claim anything from you in exchange, yet who is gratified when we come to the emotional comfort that is so fundamental in the bad days.

They are worth gratitude, warmth, inclination and joy.

They are worth being honestly and courageously honored, rewarded and thanked.

Some relevant questions that can help you better know your friend?

1. Do you have a secret that you did not tell me?

We have all kept a secret that we will not share with anyone. If he tells you, you have a lot of confidence.

2. What scares you?

To confess someone's fears is also a sign of trust. If you open your heart, you can be sure that you are important to him.

3. Where would you go on vacation?

This question is interesting in case one day you decide to go with him somewhere. In this way, you will know more or less if you share the same tastes as you.

4. What would be your dream job?

The work is very personal, and it's a very important part of the person's life. When you work on what you love, you are happy.

5. Do you have a favorite book? What is it?

In the books a person reads, it is also possible to know what worries them. An adventure book, a psychology book. Let's see what your friend answers.

6. What does freedom mean to you?

This is one of those existential questions that will give you information about what your values are and what you think about freedom.

7. If you dominated the world, what would you do to change it?

If your friend is a critical thinking person, has a good heart and is interested in social issues, definitely have some ideas for the world to work better.

8. What qualities do you value most in someone?

This question can be very personal, but it will undoubtedly help you to know your friend better and to share his comments on what he likes and dislikes.

9. How do you see the future?

Visualizing the future in one way or another provides information about someone's aspirations, motivation and even self-confidence.

There are people who prefer the mountains, because they like to ski, for example. Instead, there are people who prefer the sun and the beach.

10. Do you identify with a song?

The music makes us feel very strong emotions and it is something very personal, which differs from one person to another.

11. What is your favorite movie? Why ?

Like musical tastes or series, movies can also provide information about their tastes. For example, if you like movies of love or horror.

12. How would you describe me?

How your friend sees you can be interesting. Do not be surprised if your idea of you is not the same as your friend's. However, if it's your friend, it's because of something.

13. Do you have a model to follow?

Everyone has someone who has marked it, or we have someone we would like to look like.

A way to know how he would like to be.

14. Is there something you think others think and that is not true?

Your friend may think that others do not know what he really is or have a bad image of him.

A question similar to the previous one, although in this case we were talking about a different facet of education, the method that is followed.

15. If you were an animal ... what would you be?

This question can reveal what your friend looks like and what virtues or flaws stand out for him.

16. Who is the most important person in your life?

The answer to this question cannot mean anything special either; but it can provide useful information in some cases, for example if your parents have separated.

17. What was the best moment of your life?

We all go through good and bad times in life. Some of them we will remember forever.

18. In what situations would you be willing to lie?

We all lied at one point, it's normal for humans. Surely, before this question, you will want to show a positive image of yourself. But I can confess what you really think.

19. How would you define your sense of humor?

Logically, there are people with more humor than others, and there is also a lot of humor, black humor, the absurd.

You probably know the sense of humor of your friend, especially if he makes jokes. Although he may be a rather serious person, you should ask him questions about this topic.

20. What talent would you like to have?

People, we have our virtues and our faults and sometimes we want things we cannot have.

21. What are you most proud of in this life?

There are moments in a person's life that make one feel very happy for what they have accomplished. Ask your friend to share this special moment with you.

22. And ... what do you regret the most?

The same thing can happen with the most unpleasant moment. It's good to open your heart and tell you.

23. What are your greatest virtue and your greatest fault?

A good question to know the image your friend has of him, both in the good and in the bad.

CHAPTER 10

FAMILY

The family is a group of people united by kinship, it is the most important organization that can belong to the man.

This union may be formed by consanguineous ties or by a legally constituted and socially recognized bond, such as marriage or adoption.

The family is the fundamental component of any society, where each individual, united by blood ties, manages to project and develop.

It is in this family context that childhood and coexistence begin, where men and women acquire skills and values that will help them overcome and reproduces these principles as they form their own families.

The family is the most general social organization, but also the most important for men.

Either by social ties, legally consecrated or by blood ties, belonging to a grouping of this.

The relationship can occur at different levels. This means that not everyone in a family has the same proximity or the same type of relationship.

Within these levels, as to illustrate the underlined, we can talk about:

- *Nuclear family*
  We refer to the group consisting of father, mother and children.

- *Extended family*
  It is composed of grandparents on sides, uncles, cousins and who corresponds.

- *Composite families*
  Which are those formed by the father and mother, and in turn with a member who has no blood relationship with one of them.

Importance of the family

The family is the fundamental core of society, and as such the entity that will contribute to the integral development of the person both physically, intellectually and spiritually. It is therefore clear that family welfare is vital for human development.

The United Nations recognizes and affirms the importance of the family as a privileged place for education, and for the purpose of raising awareness of family issues.

The family is where we are born and grow, we find protection and security, and it is the cell where people respond to their needs for protection, companionship, food and health care.

The family is responsible for encouraging the child to develop as a member of a social group, with a sense of belonging, with the ability to understand and respect the culture of his group.

The influence of parents is essential. The child learns who he is from his relationship with his parents. Nobody can discover if there is no context of love and appreciation.

Sociologists argue that there are three rings for the formation of the person: the family, the school and society.

Today, the family makes up the ring that has more power. It is the one that absorbs the other two rings.

The importance of the family is that it is the first group to which an individual belongs, so it is the first group where rules, thoughts, customs and reactions are learned; The family is an institution where values, behaviors and basic education are learned, such as those usually released by the family unit.

The family is the basic unit of society; its nature, functions and contributions are recognized as fundamental to the economic and social development of nations.

Strong, healthy and sustainable families are derived from strong, healthy and sustainable societies.

On the contrary, a weakening of family structures and dynamics has an adverse impact on society, causing problems affecting indicators of well-being of household members, especially minors.

Our family is a very important part of our lives. It helps us to improve our personality and shape our character.

It teaches us the value of love, affection, affection, honesty and self-confidence, and provides us with the tools to succeed in life.

The family is a place where you can be yourself. It is a place where you are accepted as you are.

This is where you are free of tension and everyone is there to help you. The family encourages you when you are surrounded by problems.

They help you survive in difficult times and fill your life with joy and happiness.

CHAPTER 11

PROCRASTINATION

The main factor that forces someone to prosper is called procrastination.

Procrastination, the art of leaving things to tomorrow. An anomaly becomes common practice, in which one is strong.

Procrastination is a real weight for professionals. In a way, it annihilates existence and encloses us in an illusion, constantly thinking about what we must achieve, without discovering the courage to solve it.

Procrastination indicates an ability to delay, push back to the next day, to back down, tasks that we should perform right away. Procrastination, a complicated, multifaceted and multifactorial manifestation, is an insightful but challenging operation on impulsive dynamics.

The aptitude which concerns us indicates an attitude which is refashioned in time, a general attraction, which can become a custom and place us in an unfortunate situation from which we cannot escape.

Procrastination is commonly known as the disease of action. When we enter into a mechanism of procrastination, we experience an uninterrupted inner struggle between the part of us who wants, who is aware that we have to put ourselves in it, and the part of us that thwarts.

To procrastinate is to put opposition to action face to face. Now, according to the principle of inertia, the first of Newton's three laws, and in a very metaphorical way, a body at rest will rest, and a body in action will continue in action.

You will then need more vigor and energy to put you in action, to get out of the inertia however once launched, the energy that you will be asked to stay in action will be much lower and stay in motion, in action, will be practical.

Procrastination is one of those suicidal and masochistic habits that separate us from our goals and happiness.

Even though we know what is good for us, we undertake to generate plans that disadvantage us and to do the opposite of our own advantage, to stifle our best determinations.

We undoubtedly know what path to take, yet we pursue the wrong path, as if we were locked up, caught up in our bad customs, as if, decidedly, we were not completely free of our actions.

Change causes panic. All changes, even positive, engender a form of anxiety. This is probably the reason why our efforts often fail, because they only increase our fear of change.

When we meditate on procrastination, we naturally evoke a person lying on his couch who chooses to have a good time and hang out instead of getting to work. On the other hand, contrary to what we could simply think, procrastination has nothing to do with laziness.

Individuals who procrastinate would even be preferably active and well organized, with what they love to achieve, what they master and what is valuable to them.

They only choose one movement to the detriment of another, which they consider referring to a later moment.

No one is born procrastinator; one becomes it, all the time, especially during the studies. It is not in any way a trait of genetic particularity that spreads from generation to generation.

If you see yourself as a habitual procrastinator, remove worry, your descendants will not necessarily become procrastinators. However, they will be easier by the example you give them. It is then an acquired and not innate character.

Procrastination is a very common skill, more cognitive than pathological, that can affect all of us.

It is then a question of a rather arbitrary attitude, which transforms us into individuals in their own right, with qualities and also faults, feelings of lust, aspirations, ups and downs of energy.

Procrastination can, of course, be a real disadvantage and create enormous complexities, with sometimes negative effects.

Procrastination is a difficulty that reaches a large number of areas, such as finance, health, even at the collective level, the management of ecological crises, however it is also an illusion for the student or the high school student, mainly when he is delivered to himself, required to study and return his homework.

The preference for quick gratification is not the only origin of procrastination, other serious aspects are to be highlighted.

The act of postponing the actions to be carried out is very close to a principle which is a priori very far from it, self-confidence.

Roughly, this ultimate becomes in opposite proportion to the product of self-confidence and the importance of the task.

If you are insured, but give no value to the work to be done, you will procrastinate again. If you give value to the job, however, have no faith in yourself, it's not going to be terrible either.

And if you do not enjoy your work or yourself, there are no comments.

One of the essential aspects that drive procrastination is anxiety. Delivering an action until tomorrow is a synonym for avoidance, which removes the stress associated with it.

Depending on the situation, this anxiety may be related to the ambiguity, to any other fear produced by the action to be performed or its possible effects.

It can particularly be a social anxiety, for example for appointments that are referred or for purposes that have a considerable collective dimension.

Do not get around the set of difficulty at first, do not know how long it will take and especially not have prior experience of the same task and then its completion create major obstacles to the prelude to action, essentially when one lacks self-confidence.

Thus, whenever we have the opportunity between a perplexed action where we risk sinking and an action that we control, we will prefer the second inevitably.

Always wants to do things in a sublime way, to testify to one's own value of which one is really suspicious, suddenly produces an unfortunate situation from which one cannot get out, being too demanding inevitably leads to not succeeding it, which ends to further damage one's image of oneself.

This race to perfection keeps us on a leash, and it can also outright create procrastination, instead of facing a probable bankruptcy, we favor, even without really realizing it, not to try at all.

The aspect of time is fundamental in procrastination, because we are continually late.

Affected individuals usually have a hard time estimating the amount of time an action can take, with an honest ability to underestimate the time required, and overstating the time remaining before the ultimate limit.

It may sound like an excess of optimism, or even someone who does not measure the danger, with the presentiment of the delay that we start to catch, we choose not to think about it and not to face the reality.

False requirements are another form of trap that also develops the firming of procrastination. Instead of embarking on a serious and late task, we choose another, less serious yet more accessible.

This with an allegation helping to get rid of the feeling of guilt. And, from false requirements to false requirements, essential things are put back on a non-existent date.

Finally, the last aspect of procrastination is, incredibly, a tendency to hyperactivity. When this one is in disorder, with real attention problems as in some children but also among a large number of adults, the danger is not to be able to create a continuous action from beginning to end.

Failure to fix one's attention leads one to continually pass from one subject to another, and in this way accomplish no task entirely.

The affected people are then lost in many actions, started but suspended, and do not recover there. This tendency to disorder and lack of concentration is certainly defeated by all the encouragement to distraction, coming mainly from different screens and other digital devices.

Just as it is useless to choose to start a diet from one hour to the next, the great decision to stop procrastinating right now is futile and more counterproductive.

Without an arrangement or a plan of action, you may fail very quickly, demoralize yourself by incriminating yourself and not be able to face the problem for a long time. You have to go from a method that will not happen to a method based on reasoning.

Understanding change involves dissecting one's own attitudes, being sure of one's motives, and setting goals based on a fairly rigorous process. You may have late assignments in various fields, work, study, do-it-yourself, filing papers, paying bills, storing clothes or books, etc.

Make a list of priorities by adopting the following two elements, the degree of urgency and utility of the task to be performed on the one hand, and the level of difficulty and difficulty on the other hand.

The element to prioritize is the degree of utility and urgency, since walking on these topics can simplify your life, and in particular will strengthen your motivation and your self-confidence if you succeed.

Then prefer the actions that you push back by old date, even if you do not have a mandatory deadline determined by external clauses.

If there are various, adopt the second criterion to order them, first those who should ask you the least effort and time, then the others.

Another necessary aspect in the fight against procrastination is the segmentation of problems. Impossible to complete a work of great importance and great complication the first time and on a short time.

It is essential to separate the heaviest actions into more accessible sub-actions, taking less time and gathering fewer problems when they are discussed one after the other.

It is necessary to admit bonuses when you achieve objectives, things that you do not give you permission to do until you have completed the agreement. This self-gratification may seem a bit simple or common, but it certainly works to maintain motivation.

From beginning to end, you risk being slowed down even by your perfection requirement or at least your desire to do well. We have seen that this aptitude, worthy in principle, can be a real venom of action.

So you have to rise to chase it behind any criticism of yourself, or behind any attempt to renounce action or pursue a task.

You will not be able to do everything exactly, it is admitted, but all that will be done will be a step towards your happiness. Be hard with your exaggerated concern for perfection.

It's better to prioritize your goals and start with the ones that matter the most while exposing the least problems, splitting the work into easier sub-actions, determining ten-minute sequences during which you do not have to do anything other than the planned work, arrange your activities according to the skills you are experiencing, especially the days or times when you are commonly the most successful, go into emergency mode when obstacles hinder, determining yourself a deadline mandatory not to be exceeded.

Try to delineate the times of the day in which you are usually the most successful. We all look a little different, some work efficiently early in the morning, others at night or at certain times of the day.

Try to give importance to these specificities to organize your activities requiring the most energy.

You may have already noticed that your performance is clearly increased when you have to accurately postpone work before a mandatory date, or when a deadline is coming to you for practical reasons.

These are periods when all our energy and our motivation are centralized on a single goal, with a notion of urgency forcing a certain precipitation.

This is why some people end up, in a more or less decided and lucid way, by getting into the habit of working at the last moment to gain efficiency.

But it is possible to duplicate this pressure by tasks that one inflicts on oneself, to constrain oneself to finish such work precisely before such a date, considering that it surpasses all the rest.

This goes through a narrower schedule than you would naturally tend to grant.

This method can bring a lot, however it is better not to overdo it because it can cause a level of exhaustion and undue stress.

Immobility is to be rejected. Put yourself into action according to a program of activities to improve things.

CHAPTER 12

ENTREPRENEURSHIP

To undertake is to get going. To be able to dream a project that suits us that make us shiver and in which we want to invest. It is being able to use a certain amount of things, actions and willingness to execute this project. Whatever the sector in which one wishes to launch.

It is the individual who is at the heart of the action of entrepreneurship and it is she, with her aptitudes, her privileges, her luminous zones and her shadowy areas that will transmit her color to the company that 'she will set up.

One can certainly find in each entrepreneur, self-management, imagination, attention, initiative, a certain aspect of an adventurous person and also the team spirit and the desire for commitment. This is the foundation of the entrepreneurial spirit that can be said to be the ability to go from a simple concept to a palpable project. It is then essential to know who have is, to have learned to relativise on its instructions for use, its weaknesses and strengths.

The entrepreneur seizes opportunities however he needs to have means as well defined technical abilities. The entrepreneur has the sense of urgency because when an opportunity presents itself, he wants to go right away. In this phase of its character, the entrepreneur may be frowned upon in an already established business since the activities are already tied up and evolve and there is fear of risk.

In fact, an opportunity evokes the fact of putting something back into action, generates a breakthrough innovation that is different from novelty. Innovation is distinctive in that its marketing and technology objective is dominant.

Entrepreneurship is a broad concept and can be perceived narrowly or broadly. Strictly speaking, entrepreneurship is the generation of wealth and employment through the act of creating or reviving a business. In the broad sense, entrepreneurship is the ability to materialize an idea, to start the project, which can lead, among other things, to the birth of a company, but it can also lead to intrapreneurship (Action to act as an entrepreneur by working in an organization in which you are employed) as a greater employability (Individual ability to acquire and maintain the skills necessary to find or keep a job, adapt to new forms of work).

To succeed in a business, everything does not depend only on the idea; it must also be considered if there is a good opportunity before boarding. As a person we can possess various ideas that abound in our mind. In the entrepreneurial process, there is what is called the opportunity assessment, which helps to analyze the most favorable ideas to accomplish.

The majority of entrepreneurs have a process of evaluating opportunities however generally they have the opportunity to elucidate things in their head or implicitly have a process of accomplishing the idea.

It is very common to hear that the entrepreneur loves risk, in fact it's wrong. What the entrepreneur does is that he sets what he is willing to compromise in the process.

The other fundamental aspect is to start where we are with what we have since the means are limited. The entrepreneur must be able to influence his environment, a whole social network of individuals who will enlist after him. When you see successful companies, it's not just because of sales, it's because they are able to attract a lot of people around their products and services. There are people, employees, customers, investors, people who order the product again, and so on.

One might think that these people come originally from the money however when starting a project there is not enough financial means. The entrepreneur will have to fantasize and fill people with enthusiasm about his product or service.

- Jim Ratcliffe of Ineos is very clear about the meaning of entrepreneurship for him:

"It's all about courage," he says. "You must have the courage of your convictions. It's easy to keep your head down and go unnoticed, but if you want to make a difference, you have to defend what you believe in, get out of the woods and expect to be shot from time to time. One must be proactive and actively seek change instead of becoming a victim of the circumstances. "

- "An entrepreneur is an individual who has the courage to realize his dreams, to ignore the risks and to use his full creative potential to innovate."
Valérie Bellavance
General manager, Quebec
Canadian Youth Business Foundation (FCJE)

- «An entrepreneur is a person who takes action.»
Josée Cusson
Director of Operations
Canadian Youth Business Foundation (FCJE)

- «An entrepreneur is someone who sees opportunities and solutions where others see problems, and then knows how to seize those opportunities.»
Christian Bélair
General manager
Grouping of young chambers of commerce in Quebec (RJCCQ)

- «An entrepreneur is someone who initiates change for a better life.»
Réjean Parent
President
Centrale des syndicats du Québec (CSQ)

- «To become an entrepreneur is to give oneself the freedom to surpass oneself.»
Louis Jacques Filion
Professor
Rogers-J.-A.-Bombardier Chair of Entrepreneurship
HEC Montréal

- *« An entrepreneur :*

- *It is someone who is carried by a vision and who wants to make a project, then a company.*
- *It is someone who "feels" a need in the market and wants to bring something new.*
- *He is an optimist who believes in himself.*
- *Prefers to go into the pile than to get lost in too complicated analyzes.*
- *He's an impatient and it's never going fast enough for him.*
- *He is a brawler, who will defend his product and his service.*
- *Like to negotiate, buy and sell better than doing management.»*

Pierre Duhamel
Journalist, Speaker, Consultant - Business and Economics

Concretely, we can say that to undertake is to bring a project because any company starts with an idea. It can be a revolutionary novelty or more clearly an existing idea that we recover or from which we are inspired. This idea gives birth to products or services that can be distributed because of the implementation of a specific structure.

To undertake is to have an ambition, it is to be at the same time debonair and perseverant. It is to be determined to assume various constraints and to be ready to deviate them in order to be able to materialize one's project.

The term entrepreneurial spirit is also frequently used to indicate those visionary and creative minds that have the ability to develop a project that has first matured in their minds.

To undertake is to have a broad mind, the opening on the world generally allows discovering the small ideas which convert us into entrepreneurs. We must then get to see the desires and needs of those who encircle us, to discover what will fill them. Usually, it is necessary to conduct accurate studies (especially market analyzes, business plans, marketing studies) before embarking without thinking. This helps to ask the right questions and prevent strategic errors.

For the entrepreneur is a utopian who wishes to advance, to produce, to invent, to initiate; who is not afraid of risk. Undertaking is a forecast of profitability and a potential that is expressed in money.

The entrepreneur is a rational, who loves numbers. To be entrepreneurial is to pursue performance by projecting and classifying jobs and appointments.

The entrepreneur is a planner who is keen to plan, organize and control.

The entrepreneur is a relationship person who loves to listen, exchange and communicate.

Why undertake?

1- Gratitude

Your family, your friends, and before long your children, will be enthusiastic about your professionnal event conducted with audacity and enthusiasm. You will provide them with the proof, the example of the success made possible by the work and the individual compromise.

2- Freedom

You are your boss, you decide on your agenda, your remuneration, and your business and with whom you will collaborate.

3- Control of your future

Founding and running your business certainly involves some risk, but in exchange you are not dependent on unemployment from above. Only the consumer is your mentor and you know how to harmonize with his changes.

4- Creation

During your professional life you will generate jobs, establish collaborators, and join partnerships with other companies, associations, institutions. You are an artist of the economic and social life.

5- Personal development

You absolutely sit in a job that you have elected. You lead a real adventure of which you are the superman; you must design solutions, overcome challenges and also experience the pride of the winner.

6- Opening to the world

Your job is not limited to your country of residence. You move to learn and see other countries, markets, techniques, cultures and horizons. You are in the midst of the trends of the global economy of our century.

7- The opportunity to live well

Your income is the only reward for your ability, your efforts and the risks you take, they help you to have a standing, a quality of life that you distribute with those you adore. You cash money and it is the fruit of your merit.

CHAPTER 13

INVESTMENT

Those who work their land will have abundant food, but those who chase fantasies will have their fill of poverty.

Here are some points to consider

- The mere fact of being an employee has never helped anyone to become rich. It can contribute as a means or be periodic, however do not rely on a single fixed income to make a fortune.

- Getting rich at no turtle is like getting rich old. If you want to become rich young, you have to find the speed.
- Which leads to the fact that you have to have different sources of income and try to multiply them in volume.
- You have to earn money when you are in bed, it means that your money is working for you and not the other way around.
- You must know the diversity between assets and liabilities. Assets earn you money and liabilities make you lose.
- Increase the assets to the maximum. The passive income generated by your assets will grow exponentially if you know how to manage your money.
- Entrepreneurship is a path to wealth because income is not limited and you have control.
- If you want the snowball effect, you need to expand and expand your business quickly.

If you have an extraordinary idea and you put it in place, everything can go very fast. If you make a very good investment and you focus on your manager abilities everything can go very fast. But be determined to take risks. The entrepreneur needs financial resources to function, human resources to expand.

What is investment?

The investment is the expenditure made by the company to increase its production capacity. This increase can take two forms. The first, called damping has the purpose of substituting worn or obsolescent machines, which means surpassed by technical progress. The second is dedicated to providing new machines in order to improve the production of the company.

Investment is the activity that dreams of either maintaining or increasing the capital stock of an economic agent. For example, households invest when they buy housing, the state invests when it builds a road, and firms invest when they provide a machine. The company's capital stock is made up of machines, computers, computer software, vehicles, land, and so on. This capital helps the institution to create products or services. In business accounting, all of these assets generate fixed assets.

There are two forms of capital assets, property, plant and equipment and intangible assets. Tangible fixed assets indicate the physical part of the business, it means especially the walls and the machines; Intangible assets represent the non-physical part, ie knowledge, software, goodwill and patents. There are then two forms of investment, attached to either the tangible or the intangible asset mix. Business investment, in the same way as household consumption, is a driving force for economic growth. In other words, investing firms participate in the diffusion of technical progress and, therefore, in productivity growth.

Conversely, it is in accordance with the degree of economic development that companies choose to invest. Investment and growth interfere and this interference is one of the obstacles of economic analysis of investment.

In economics, an investment is an immediate disbursement subject to increase, in the future, the wealth of the one who commits it. The investment leads to solid growth as it simultaneously acts on demand and supply. The driving function of investment in economic demand was pronounced by Keynes. However, Keynes has particularly developed the multiplier effect of the investment which leads to a growth more powerful than its initial amount.

You must know that firstly high returns often accompany significant risks. Nobody gives you anything. If there is an opportunity to earn a lot, it is because there is also the possibility of losing a lot. Do not be greedy. You have your whole life in front of you. Act with a head, step by step and with a good foot. Do not hurry, there is time for everything. Before investing (money or anything else), train, gain knowledge, become a connoisseur on the subject, learn what you are going to do.

Invest not what you have, but what you get. Your basic needs come first. Your family comes first Do not invest what you do not have, or what you have but will soon need for important things. This obviously includes not borrowing to invest. Debt = chains, death, slavery. Do not work for them. And if you already have debts, do your best to get out. Escape those who do not offer you security, but only words. There are people who speak very well, who wear a suit and a tie and for these simple data, you think they are someone. Flee to whom you aspire only appearance. Ask for credentials, experience, security, data, numbers.

That said, and to get into the material, let's sees where you can invest money. I have been doing this for years; it is a very interesting activity, although what I am going to say here is only objective possibilities. I do not encourage or defend anything. I limit myself to expressing what I know and what I do. Do not interpret it as a push that I want to give you. It is very delicate. Everyone is free to make decisions and must experience the consequences of what he does. In any case, there are differences in profiles, countries, times ... so each case is a case.

Where to invest money?

1) Real estate

My favorite option. And yes, I know that there are real estate bubbles, risks, etc. Still, it's my favorite option, essentially for two reasons:

Real estate, especially housing, are basic goods. You will always need apartments, like bread, oil, shirts, trousers, that is to say, there will always be people who will buy them, because there will always be people who will need to live under a roof. There are many opportunities for investment and profit-making. You are not doomed to one thing. You can rent the property or resell it to realize a capital gain.

By real estate, we have a wide variety of assumptions, mainly:

- Housing, as we said, so that people can live. You rent them, you sell them later.
- Commercial premises, for businesses, businesses, which tend to be more expensive than housing.
- Rustic land, which offers the advantage that its tax burden is lower than real estate. Another advantage is that you can develop an agricultural activity by entrusting their management and work to third parties, with whom you have a fully operational activity.

As I said at the beginning, it's my favorite option when it comes to investing money. The risk is low and the returns and opportunities for profits very reasonable. Volatility is also rare. There may be price variations, but they occur in relatively long cycles, that is, they can be seen coming, not like we are going to see now.

2) Stock Markets

Another interesting option IF YOU KNOW WHAT YOU DO (Emphasis in capital letters).

I am in favor of learning a method and following it. Nothing to try, act according to what the specialized press says, let you be guided by someone, who in turn is guided by someone. In the securities markets (stock exchanges), there are also many investment opportunities. There are people who opt for companies that offer good benefits (dividends) and others who prefer speculation (buy cheap to sell expensive). The latter has always attracted me more. You can make money not only when the stock price goes up, but also when it goes down, which is why I said there are many possibilities. If you like the risk, you have the leverage option and if, on the other hand, you do not want to warm your head, you can learn in a simple way how to invest in index funds or similar options.

3) Financial products

Strictly speaking, they refer to different numbers in which you can invest money to finance others. In other words, you have money, you need another, you are, you lend it and it uses it. This other can be a private entity, for example a business (corporate bonds) or a public entity, if you are so innocent that you think the state spends what it collects in taxes, and I have to get you out of there.

Error: the state spends what it removes (taxes), what you indebted, what you have, what you do not have and what you put in front of you. States and governments are true financial predators; it happens to them as at the bank, they never have enough. In the broad sense, when we talk about financial products, we refer to any type of product that gives us a return for our money. This would also include, for example, retirement plans.

4) Startups

Startups are technology companies, which burst with new business models to meet new needs (or to create them), and for this reason they lack references for their valuation. It's a pure risk, there is nothing that can help you set parameters. They can start from sorrow or harvest incredible successes.

I must admit that before them I meet a curious contradiction, I am not a risk lover but I am strongly attracted, in fact I am an investor in several of them. It's strange, I love the vision that some people have of designing business and projects in a world as changeable as ours, the ability to anticipate the future and perhaps the desires of people. It fascinates me so much that sometimes I invest. Now, I've said it before, I'm investing what I do not need, and if I lose, it will not negatively affect any aspect of my life.

5) Crowdlending

Crowdlending is a variant of crowdfunding. If you do not know what is neither, I will tell you:

- Crowdfunding is a form of investment that involves paying money to many people, usually in small amounts, to a project or business that is ongoing or will be born.
- Crowdending is a form of investment that involves lending money between people to one another or to others. It would become the substitute or the modern and democratic alternative to the bank.

The crowdlending is very good. The profits are quiet, we do not cheat, but you have your money there, producing a return without having to do much. A crowdlending modality is financing companies through different loan formulas, for example promissory note discounts. When a company receives a promissory note from someone and has to get it back in the future, if you need the money before you can deduct the document, collect it in advance and pay interest in exchange. There are platforms that facilitate these operations and in which you can invest the money.

Investment rules

- Invest in a long-term vision

"*Our favorite period of detention is forever.*» Warren Buffett (American investor and philanthropist)

A predictor who saves money with a long-term vision in order to be able to react to hard times, is much more likely to achieve his ends than the one who seeks to speculate on the market in hunting gains snapshots. The longer you invest, the higher the starting value of your investment is to enjoy the effect of capitalization. A large number of investors are already accustomed to the concept of capitalization via their savings account. Capitalization is the mechanism by which interests manage to add to your initial investment and, in turn, generate other interests. In the long run, it can make a big difference, as long as you invest your profits again.

- Take into account valuations

Whichever method you prefer to invest, it is essential not to pay more than the essentials for the sustainability of a company's earnings or development visions. It's all about patience. We must hope that the best opportunity arises.

We are convinced that investing your money in a good company at an adequate price can generally be confirmed wiser than investing in a decent company at a good price.

- Focus on the concrete result

Inflation, taxes and fees indicate three items that may have a negative effect on the actual rate of return on your investment. There are some alternatives to help reduce costs, especially inflation-defensive tools, such as inflation-linked bonds (securities designed to help investors protect themselves from inflation). Another option is corporate real estate, where rents are generally magnified at the same rate as inflation so that prices rise.

- Diversify your risks

Having a deferred portfolio of unrelated investments can reduce risk compared to investing in a single asset or market, as well as other less sensitive risks such as inflation, which can have the effect of deteriorating the value of the assets in case of acceleration. Equities, bonds (debt instruments usually designed by a company or a state, at a generally fixed interest rate and for a given duration, at the end of which the debt is returned), real estate and liquid assets react otherwise in relation to market conditions. Adopting various asset classes can help to avoid seeing the value of all your investments go up or down at the same time. Geographic diversification also helps to diversify risks. Investing in investments such as UCITS can also solve many of the challenges of managing a huge portfolio. Finally, and especially, any investor must determine a degree of risk where he feels comfortable with his investment vision.

- Do not join the crowd

"Be fearful when others are greedy. Be greedy when others are fearful." Warren Buffett (American investor and philanthropist)

As we have seen from the snowball effect in 2008, following the crash of the US investment bank Lehman Brothers, fortuitous or fatal news can have significant effects on equity market developments. Of course, a large number of defensive companies, producing significant cash flows and able to generate value in different market conditions, have generally suffered the same negative sentiment that has led to the decline in share prices of companies more sensitive to economic conditions and of lower quality.

- Invest in what you control

"Investment in knowledge is the one that brings the most interest." Benjamin Franklin (one of the founding fathers of the United States of America, 1706-1790)

If a well-established portfolio can be the cause of consistent performance for an investor, the opposite is also true. It is child's play to make unavoidable losses by putting money into an asset that is not performing as intended. It is imperative for any saver to take the time of reflection in order to be sure to understand what he wants to have.

- Dodge the overconfidence

The antecedent does not prejudge in any way how an investment could be in the future and investors should try to appreciate the possible risks associated with a specific investment with its potential profits. The value of the investments may fluctuate and may also reduce or improve the net asset value of the funds. You cannot recover your initial investment. Please note that past performance does not prejudge future performance. Be aware that the value of your investment may go down as well as up due to currency fluctuations.

PART 3

THE FOUR (4) KEY STEPS TO GETTING OUT OF DEBT

CHAPTER 14

BE HEALTHY

According to the WHO (World Health Organization) definition, health refers to a state of complete well-being, including physical, mental, social, environmental status. So health is not just about being sick or having a disability. It is a relative concept, felt by each individual. No concrete measure can measure health, since health is the fact of satisfying all its needs (emotional, nutritional, relational, health ...). In medicine, health is the absence of disease.

We must therefore avoid wanting to assess the state of well-being, therefore health of an individual from our own experience of life. We may not understand the life of others, especially when it is very far from our criteria, it does not mean that the person is in poor health so far.

According to the clarification of health provided by WHO we can say that when we start not feeling good in our life, we turn away from health and we start to take the path of the arrival of signs of disease.

The physical health condition is calculated using data that is proportional to the diseases and traumas that disturb all systems of the human body, respiratory, digestive, nervous, reproductive, and so on. Incipient events within a population, such as epidemics, can also be taken into account.

Mental health and psychosocial status is measured through positive mental health data, social adjustment difficulties involving various types of violence, neglect and abuse, social integration and the growth of the child.

What to do to be healthy?

Be healthy especially means not to be sick. Being healthy means feeling good, all over one's body and in society. Our daily behavior will help a lot. Here are some essential points and rules to keep you healthy:

1- Have a lot of physical activity. To stay healthy our body needs frequent physical activity. Walking for fun, biking, climbing the stairs on foot, playing sports, all activities beneficial for children and adults alike.

Our breathing rate and pulse should increase for at least half an hour daily. Children need to move a lot and do it with pleasure.

2- To be happy and serene. Our inner happiness and serenity are strengths that also allow us to face the problems of life. Despite our balance and serenity are influenced by external factors, we are however the first responsible. If we hope that other people give us a feeling of happiness, it makes us subject.

3- Eat in a healthy way. Eating in a healthy way does not just mean feeding enough. Balanced nutrition is essential to keeping our body healthy. For our happiness, it is necessary to eat daily fruits and vegetables and drink a lot of unsweetened drinks.

Avoid as much fat and sugar as they are bad for our body. If what we have in our plate is essential, a beautiful atmosphere at the edge of the family table is also. Children must also know how to eat in a healthy way. So, they need the example of parents and their advice.

4- Be part of a family. It can strengthen the feeling of security and happiness. Whether it is a small family or a large family, each individual has his own personality. For family life to be perfect, mutual understanding and respect are essential.

5- Have friends. We also need, apart from our family, people we feel comfortable with, trust, laugh about and support when we have difficulties. Good contacts with other people are not always done through words. You can also express yourself with a smile or a sympathetic gesture.

6- Have enough money to live. The world tends to merge money and happiness. We think that being able to provide such and such a thing would make us happy. Money is not everything. On the other hand, we are happy to have enough money to acquire what is needed from day to day.

If this is not the case, the social service of the municipality or a budget advisory service can provide assistance. In our world, children and adolescents are also always encouraged to consume.

With our support and the example we give them, they learn to determine their priorities and to recognize the limits.

7- Have dreams and ambitions. Our dreams and ambitions often help us escape from everyday life. They belong to our inner world. They can also inspire us to make a difference in our lives. When dreams and ambitions take up too much space in our lives, they want to prevent us from observing the good things of our daily life that are worth being enjoyed, improved and supported.

Sometimes we teach our children dream that we have not been able to achieve ourselves. This can make their growth difficult and overload their path in life. Our children need to have their own dreams and must discover their own way in life.

8- Allow yourself moments of relaxation. Family, children, work, perhaps annoyances or homesickness, this entire can cause a lot of stress and pressure. It is therefore necessary to allow you a break from time to time and to have some moments of relaxation. It is not enough to hope that pressure and stress disappear.

It is better to deliberately seek relaxation and rest. The first step is to take a daily time for this, even if it is only some minutes. For example to go for a walk, sing, dance, read, take a bath, breathe well, and take a nap.

9- Live my sexuality adequately. Sexuality is a very intimate domain. Every human being lives his sexuality in a different way and according to other needs. Sexual relations should not be considered as a duty, however, a source of relaxation. A proper sexuality is also made of soft words and gestures, of time, attention and consideration, towards one's partner as well as oneself.

Otherwise, the risk is to omit one's own needs and desires and not to preserve one's physical and psychic health. To protect you from AIDS in a relationship, spouses must be faithful or protect themselves by using condoms.

10- Have a suitable job. Whether working at home as a housewife and stay-at-home mom or having a professional activity, the joy that one finds in one's work derives not only from what one achieves, but also from one's own behavior. Often our desires are far from reality. It is not easy, however, getting irritated at this point does not progress anything.

It's best to think about how to increase your chances in the job market. Surely a course to better communicate the local language or other continuing education could be appropriate.

11- Sleep enough. The number of hours of sleep needed to feel relaxed in the morning changes from person to person. He leads to take his own needs seriously and to adjust his sleep, sleep pace given the situation. Stress, noise and light can make sleep worse.

Watching provocative or disturbing movies can hurt sleep, especially in children. Regular bedtime and small rituals before bedtime allow adults and children to sleep well.

12- Prevent stress. Stress is very fatal for health. It causes migraines and can produce heart problems, among others. Stress is destroyed in every way and it is mandatory to fight against this stress.

   To do this, you have to learn how to pick up, relax and breathe.

CHAPTER 15

FIND HAPPINESS

- Aristotle: "Happiness is the happy life and the happy life is the virtuous life."

- Socrates: "Happiness is pleasure without remorse."

- Jules Barbey d'Aurevilly: "Happiness is the happy life and the happy life is the virtuous life."

- Somerset Maugham: "Happiness is the happy life and the happy life is the virtuous life."

- André Maurois: "Happiness is never immobile; happiness is the respite in anxiety. »

- Groucho Marx: "Money does not make happiness, and that's absolutely true, but it's a pretty good thing to own in a home."

- Jean-Jacques Rousseau: "There is no happiness without courage, nor virtue without combat."

- Sigmund Freud: "Happiness is a childhood dream realized in adulthood."

- Confucius: "All men think that happiness is at the top of the mountain while it resides in the way of climbing."

- Seneca: "One cannot be happy when one lives only for oneself, when one brings everything back to one's own interest. We really live for ourselves only by living for another. "

- Antoine de Saint-Exupery: "If you want to understand the word happiness, you have to hear it as a reward and not as a goal."

- Saint Luke: "There is more happiness to give than to receive"

- Voltaire: "Happiness is often the only thing we can give without having it and it is by giving it that we acquire it."

- Jean de La Fontaine: "Neither gold nor greatness makes us happy."

According to Kant, happiness cannot be developed by words. We cannot express with conviction what will make us happy, because for that we would need a complete understanding of ourselves and the world. To be happy is not an abstract of reason but an abstract of the imagination.

Happiness can be created in two distinct ways, either as a real feeling, or as an abstract conception. In the first way, happiness would then be concrete, perceived, a kind of pleasure, he would experience. In the second way, happiness would not be experienced in the immediate future, it would be preferably a sentence carried late, on his life.

If happiness is a sentence, it can also be imagined in many ways. First, as a sentence to consider whether we have been good or bad, whether or not we can feel happy, it means whether we are lucky or not. It also challenges the origin of the word happiness (happiness, good luck: "heur" means "luck" in Old French, and also currently in the language have the chance to: "I have no time to please him and some languages (luckily, luckily).

This is how we will be happy, for example, if we came out alive from a plane crash, even if we are paralyzed for life, even if we suffer in the body (and that one cannot then find happiness in the sense of an experience, of a feeling).

It can also be said that happiness is a sentence, since all sensation is painful, only pain and misery would be experienced, happiness, on the contrary, would be nothing positive, it would only indicate the lack of unhappiness or pain. This is, for example, Schopenhauer's opinion.

Finally, happiness will also be a sentence if we imagine it not as entertainment however as the triumph or the pleasure of having acted well, there is also a sentence on our antecedent.

Therefore, according to the Stoics, happiness is limited to virtue, the virtuous man, who acts well, is happy.

It is not a question here of a feeling (the Stoic opinion of happiness concerns exactly to present that one can be happy in pain), however, contrary to a sentence on our previous action, on its virtuous quality. On the possibility that we had to overcome our abilities and our desires and to do well.

We observe that the difference between lived and sentence corresponds with the difference between abstract and concrete, and also with the difference between relative and absolute, more precisely, if happiness is mastered, it is something won, complete in the sense that it does not flow from anything else; however, if our happiness is a sentence that confronts our destiny with that of others or with a median spell (which it was wisely allowed to wait), then happiness arises from a rapprochement, it is relative.

The contrast between happiness and pleasure can be seen in two ways, we can see that happiness is lasting, while pleasure is momentary. However, sometimes we express a moment of happiness, and we do not want to just express a moment of pleasure, which differentiates then, beyond duration, the happiness of pleasure, it is the concept that happiness is more complete, that it indicates an entire well-being of the body and the mind, while the pleasure only looks at the body.

We can also emphasize that all feeling seems momentary, since we have, for example, knowledge of evolution, for example, in a show, our eye is prompted by what moves; also, many times one only becomes aware of a sound when it stops, or when it starts; also, one can conceive that all sensations are momentary, whereas pleasure is the consciousness of an evolution.

It would be ascertained that pleasure cannot be long-lasting, since any feeling which is prolonged happens to be silenced, one gets used to it.

For example, the man adapts himself to the pain (the patient manages not to think about his / her / its evil) as well as to the pleasure (once cured, it will be entertained in the first times, however after a few days it will not have more aware of his contentment). Pleasure and happiness could only subsist in evolution, and from their opposites (pain and misfortune).

If the feeling is mainly differential, then we have the freedom to choose between experiencing great pleasures interrupted by great suffering, or living a state of lasting well-being, however, which seems to us bland and would be experienced without great pleasure.

Happiness is strictly attached to desire, of course, is the subject at the highest point of desire not happiness? And does not happiness constitute the satisfaction of our desires? We will then begin to study the links between happiness and desire.

Happiness is in the satisfaction of our desires, such is the hedonistic opinion. Hedonism refers to the notion that pleasure is the extreme value, the goal of life, which distinguishes happiness and pleasure.

Now, pleasure is considered as that which escorts the satisfaction of all desire; then happiness will be manifested, for the hedonist, by the satisfaction of desires.

We can identify two fundamental versions of the hedonistic hypothesis; there are those who attest that happiness is defined as fulfilling all our desires, and those who advocate seeking to fill only some desires.

Happiness is in the limitation of our desires, as the Stoic theory says.

Of course, if happiness is the satisfaction of our desires, this satisfaction can be achieved in two ways, by combining the world with our desires, it means trying to discover what we want, by combining our desires with the world it means looking to desire what one has.

This reversal of sight is miraculous; it seems to achieve complete happiness, whatever the case may be. However, it does not go without complications.

Happiness is in the annihilation of desire, such is the pessimistic opinion. One could also say that, for the pessimists, there is just no happiness. By pessimistic, I indicate in particular the philosophy of Buddha (who gave birth to the Buddhist religion) and that of Schopenhauer.

Happiness is in the evolution of desires; such could be an opinion of happiness based on the notion of sublimation. Of course, sublimation indicates the fact of moving a desire towards a purpose other than its purpose of departure.

The idea is simple; the true happiness must be perennial. It is also a peculiarity that can identify the happiness of simple pleasure. We find this point of view in Aristotle.

We also find in Montaigne this point of view that we cannot judge happiness until the day of his death. Not only because one sees just the whole of his life, but also because we see his way of resisting death.

Surely, it is better to have lasting happiness than a momentary happiness. However it is easier to say than to realize.

After having determined happiness as the conquest of pleasure and bypassing suffering, Freud points out the complication of achieving lasting happiness.

> Happiness is to be sought in the present moment.

> *Let everyone examine his thoughts, he will find them all busy in the past and the future. We hardly think of the present; and, if we think about it, it is only to take the light of it to dispose of the future. The present is never our end; the past and the present are our means; the only future is our end. So we never live, but we hope to live; and, having us always to be happy, it is inevitable that we never be happy.*

> Pascal, *Pensées*, § 172

Pascal is pessimistic, and he does not think that an individual can discover happiness, not even by focusing on the present moment, since he falls into boredom; it means the pain of examining his miserable condition in the face.

However one can be little pessimistic, and judge that by omitting a little the future and concentrating more in the present moment it is likely to find happiness.

Consequently, the philosopher André Comte-Sponville affirms, in his Treatise on Despair and Bliss, that the key to happiness is to give up hope. Plato deluded himself, he said: he mixed desire and hope. The desire is not always lacking, it is the hope that is always missing, and we can want what we have, while we never hope what we have.

With this differentiation, Comte-Sponville preserves desire and rejects hope. Hope is that ridiculous desire that can only lead us to misfortune, which deviates us from our present happiness for an uncertain happiness that does not depend on us.

Finally, a large number of poets have put their art at the service of this fundamental message: carpe diem. Use the moment. Like Horace, Ovid, or Ronsard, gather the roses of life today.

Certainly, in philosophy, as long as you say something, you can be sure that you can also say the opposite.

Otherwise it would not be philosophy, however, of science. Some say that happiness is in the present, some will say that happiness is in the past. However this distinction of probable opinions should not make you fall into the relativism that says the truth is one, since the reality is one.

In philosophy, the truth is hypothetical, you must choose what you think is real.

First, if happiness is the opposite of misfortune, it necessarily results from a sentence on our past. For Schopenhauer, for example, happiness is nothing more than the remoteness of misfortune.

To find happiness is to notice that one does not suffer anymore. It is then always a sentence on our past that makes us happy, compared with our present condition. Happiness, if it exists, we have noticed that it was not clear to Schopenhauer, can then be conjugated to the present; however it is manifest only by a sentence on our past.

However, we can go further, and agree that happiness in itself is first in the past. Are not the happiest periods of our existence still more beautiful in our memory than when we live them?

Since when we live these times, we are caught in the action, and we are filled with ambiguity about the future. We do not know what will happen, or whether this happiness will continue.

So, we do not like it the same way as when we observe these same periods, once we arrive, in our memories. So all ambiguity has taken the sails, and these spectacles of our existence settle in the past, deduced to fortune, indissoluble, forever. And what a pleasure to reconsider these memories.

Our thought makes them more beautiful without stopping, the melancholy illuminates them with its curling light. We mythologize them, so that the present happiness seems very pale compared to previous happiness. Our spirit is a container, and our memories are wine, they improve as they age.

Marcel Proust also emphasizes this opinion. The whole of his work aims to recall the ravings of reminiscence, to see at once revealing his past according to the desire for a simple sensation that we are experiencing once again and which gives rise to other sensations and memories related to it in our consciousness.

However, to certify in this way that happiness is in the past, that is to say that happiness is found in reminiscence, in the memory of a little while past. It is then, to tell the truth, to the present that this happiness is experienced.

The unique hypotheses that actually put happiness in the past are eventually the different imaginary and religious opinions that represent a golden age.

For example, for Christian belief, man was only happy during the time preceding original sin that means when

Adam and Eve still enjoyed the Garden of Eden in complete tranquility.

From original sin, man is held to suffering and misery. He will probably only be able to experience happiness once again after death.

One could therefore close the picture with the opinions that put happiness in the future. This is certainly the belief of Christianity, which certifies the existence of paradise. However one could also observe this opinion in religions.

For the sociologist Marcel Gauchet, a change has taken place with modernity, religions have given way to ideologies.

While the religions classified the ideal in the past and gave the social time as a destruction or a tumble (it was then necessary to like to preserve, to honor the custom, to imitate the ascendants in an attempt to recover the lost value), the ideologies, against -current, put happiness and the goal to succeed in the future.

Social and historical time is thus understood as an improvement estimated capable of bringing us closer to this marvelous future condition, of the big night, of those humming tomorrows. This is certainly the case of communism, which predicts the coming of the end of history and of a classless society, neither state, delinquency, injustice, misfortune, etc.

However, this is also the case with liberalism, insofar as it is also an ideology that advises to make some sacrifices (admit a reduction of social assistance and a reduction of the minimum wage for example) in the name of some future goods mortgaged.

Religions express, that yesterday it was more satisfying. Ideologies say that Tomorrow will be much more satisfying. Both allow themselves to say that at present, whatever the circumstances, we are unhappy.

How to be happy?

It is useless to look for a unique formula to happiness since it also depends on each person's aspirations and personality structure.

To succeed is to build a building in three dimensions, material, relational and emotional. In other words, achieve its ends, while ensuring good relations and good representation, without losing its well-being.

A social success that would leave us unhappy is no longer considered by our contemporaries as an ideal of successful life.

But also the material and relational measures have a real logic, as much the emotional dimension of a fulfilled life, with its instinctive (our alienations) and biological (our character) airs proves more painful to experiment.

Decide to be well. It is often simpler, less expensive in psychological decision, to accept going to bad luck. On the contrary, to continue the well-being requires efforts. There are clear disparities between men in their willingness to feel good.

And elements specific to the human race. Evolution seems to have maintained in us the existence of negative feelings, of which the function is to reinforce the probabilities of conservation of the species. Anxiousness is profitable to escape or combat, anger frightens adversaries or rivals, sadness incites pity, etc.

However, nature, if she had the embarrassment of our survival, has dizzily had that of our quality of life. The shadow of positive emotions and moods is amply smaller, more fragile, and more expensive access in terms of psychological energy.

Do not leave too much room for the feeling of unhappiness. If the negative sensations are fortuitous, unstable and reasonably disturb our daily lives, we can hope that they succumb on their own. However, to baratinate with misfortune, particularly emphasized by romanticism in the nineteenth century, admits some risks that psychology will study better.

Showing a negative sensation may increase the duration. One imagined in previous periods some cathartic consequence; Lamenting would help to relieve his pain, for example. It seems that this is usually the opposite, repeated and unanswered whining can change into a martyrdom of life. And unhappiness feeds on it, the more we let ourselves go, the more we increase the duration. In addition, letting go of the feeling of unhappiness will gradually move from a regular negative emotion (one feels overwhelmed) to a perennial negative conception (one has an unfortunate life).

Finally, this facilitates the return of the negative feelings later, the fact is well absorbed in the depression, which has a very powerful disposition to the recurrence, and it has been proved with regard to the daily sad mood.

Take care of yourself, especially when you are not well. Another truth? Yes, however a thousand times challenged by observation. Most anxious and discouraged are doing exactly the opposite. The more they go wrong, the more they go wrong, no longer going out with their friends, no longer exercising their favorite hobbies.

And the more they go wrong, the worse they go. Doing pleasant activities when you are not doing well is not a matter of veracity, since you do not want to do it. However, all the available works underline that it is necessary to relaunch this desire by initial efforts, like the reinstatement of an engine which stalled.

And that we must not go wrong, when we go wrong, the goal of pleasant activities is not to help us find happiness, but to avoid the malaise of increasing or to settle.

No exaggerated concern for perfection or thought that obsesses well-being. Flaubert, eloquent in happiness, wrote: "Have you thought how much this horrible word has brought tears? Without this term, we slept more calm and we would live in a comfortable situation. (In "Dictionary of accepted ideas", Maxi-Livres, 2001).

There is no point in taking Gustave word for word, however still, the quest for happiness should not turn to monomania, and the right to well-being (figured elsewhere in the US Constitution) should not be changed on duty of well-being.

Even more so because the feeling of unhappiness, which belongs to existence, can sometimes be necessary, making us think, and making us become vigilant in the face of painful realities. We cannot defend it, but we need to make good use of it.

Faced with everyday difficulties, think, but do not think too much. The study of the psyche of the anxious indicates that they always have concerns in their head, while, surprisingly, they never approach them advantageously, their ruminations do not provide them with alternatives. It is that the call of the hassle is to be an alarm (to draw our attention to a difficulty) and not a way to see the world or face its problems.

This is the reason why one of the privileged aims of psychotherapies, especially cognitive ones, is to lead people to look at their misfortunes as difficulties to overcome and not as fatalities.

Do not feed on hostile feelings. Much of our misfortune stems from our exaggerated position on hostile feelings. They are sometimes very powerful and turned in opposition to defined people (resentment, bitterness, jealousy, etc.). Generally, they grow because we favor our need to be right (They are wrong, they must be punished) to our desire to feel good.

In other cases, these negative sensations come from susceptibility to the imperfections of the human race, and place a delicate or insolent vision on the world and its inhabitants. The absence of benevolence is generally an affirmation of ill-being, and often a source of misfortune.

Enjoy the periods of happiness. The best weapon against misfortune, and the best to use, is surely to enjoy even better the good times that the existence presents us. To appreciate happiness when it is there, to strengthen it, to increase it symbolizes a very good vaccine against the feeling of unhappiness.

You will not possibly prevent the disease; however it will be in a reduced form. As always, it's not that simple. The philosopher André Comte-Sponville expresses very clearly all the clutter that there is to find happiness when all is well. Let us not hope for the misfortune to evoke that life can be beautiful and to pity not to have better exploited it.

CHAPTER 16

GIVE AND RECEIVE

The universe is driven by a set of laws and principles. To give and to receive is a law which remains identical to itself, worthy of praise and which extends to everything. What we give comes alive and changes the one who received it. This law extends to all angles of life. As a result, life turns into a cycle.

We are going through a time when the socio-economic condition will result much more difficult this satisfaction to give and this joy to receive.

Giving is an advantage, because to be in this place, it is necessary at first to have received and to be ready to transmit. Assuredly, we can only give what we have received, yet we have all received the opposite of what we usually think. If only life.

And also the opportunity to smile, to extend a hand, to audition, to express a word of circumstance, to hug a person, to express his love, to give a kiss.

Giving is then a prescription of the heart more than a transfer of goods. So, we can all give and admit to receive. However incredibly to transmit, it is necessary at first time to be clear on what life has already given us by being as objective as possible. From this reception enchains the succession of our habit and the intensity of our happiness to give.

Giving is essential in a relationship. None of our links, whether personal or professional, can go forward and be suitable in the medium and long term if we do not continually give of ourselves, without expecting anything in return.

This donation does not have to be material; it can be granted in a smile, a listening time, understanding, affection, gratitude, a helping hand, reinforcement for a project, our participation from a talent or our ability , a homemade gift, a thank you, an attention, etc.

When we give in a healthy way, not only do we participate in doing well to each other and to the relationship, but we perceive a sense of gaining something for ourselves by maintaining the best of ourselves. This kind of gift amuses our soul and satisfies our being.

However, the act of giving is invigorating and provides an intense happiness only if it is done in the respect of our limits, the balance give-receive and without ulterior motive.

Giving is to sow and to receive, to reap. In this way, what we give comes back to life on another air. A grain sown in good soil endures new transmutations before it duplicates itself. It deteriorates, it begins to penetrate the earth, it grows gradually, it duplicates itself and gives each turn many grains.

Every good farmer continually benefits from the right moment and knows when to sow such seed or seed. He also knows that each seed is unique to its kind. Nature uses the notion of time as well as us. Nature is not inconsistent.

Nothing is immobile. Everything belongs to a system. To grasp a few things it is not enough to look at a single factor. It must be examined as a whole. An iceberg is bigger than the tip we see. One movement is the product of many. All our movements count.

Some wise men of this society find more joy to give than to receive. They devote their time to the concerns of humanity. They know when to support others.

Mother Teresa is a model, an example of charity. Everywhere she benefited the poor, the poor and the underprivileged. Throughout her life and even after her death, she is the representation of peace, love, joy and serenity.

Many are those who contribute in the necessities of humanity. On the other hand, it is the heroes and heroines in silence.

Referring to the water cycle, the rain does not fall without reacting to nature. Therefore, that entire one gives, makes a great reaction on the one who receives it. To know how to give restores the sick, delivers a nation, a life, brings back hope.

Supporting others, produces joy in the heart, provides happiness, health and the feeling of well-being.

The scriptures tell us: Whatever you want men to do for you, do the same for them. This law warns us about our understanding and our conduct towards others.

If you want us to love you, love others first. If you want us to do you good, in the first place, do well to others.

Of course, each person is the guarantor of what touches him in life. It's like a magnetic force that captivates certain things towards it.

The most important thing is that well-ordered charity begins with oneself. Love yourself as much as you can. Give yourself some time.

Be kind to yourself. And, excuse you. We do not give what we do not have. And, we do not receive what we did not give.

Our tendency to give and receive is at the heart of our experience of prosperity.

Receive and to Give are like the two facades of the same coin, the poles of the same energy that moves, such is the normal flow of existence. If one of the polarities comes to immobilize or take an unacceptable position, the whole system is troubled.

We have all received certain aptitudes or intelligences that we exploit and distribute without embarrassment because we already have them in very large quantities, and we usually receive estimation and elevation in exchange.

However, we all have shortcomings, or received too little in some other things, which gives rise to anxiety and instability between what can be received and what can be given.

I urge you to carefully observe your own stability between giving and receiving. The most common obstacle is difficulty receiving.

And this difficulty can take unimaginable ways, such as the excess of giving that ends up dry or bitter.

There are quite a few reasons that can be the cause of this, such as our cultural conditioning (giving is ethically more important than receiving) or family conditioning, and a huge platform of opinions that we hold about ourselves and the society in which we live.

To start the cycle of giving and receiving, the first step, and certainly the most useful, is to develop the language of your gratitude for what you are currently receiving.

When you take water at the source of life, even the air you breathe, and the food you absorb, you start to realize that none of this is going into stock.

It is more attractive and productive to think in relation to the flow, and not in terms of possession.

Anything you receive must be redistributed in one way or another, that's how life goes on, and we belong to that movement.

To give and to receive it can only be envisaged on the largest possible scale, when I give, it is not of this individual in particular that I hope a return.

It is life itself that is dedicated to setting in motion the flow of return.

When I give, it is the act of giving that counts, more than the thing or the service rendered. It is the relationship with our fellow men and with ourselves that we bid on, giving us the feeling of being alive, having a location and a score to perform in the grand spectacle of the universe.

Equally, accepting to receive rightly is giving the other the opportunity to give, and to experience, accordingly, one's own worth. Is not the beautiful offer you can do to him?

Restoring the balance between giving and receiving is one of the most significant keys to bringing the cycle of prosperity into motion.

One of the secrets of joy is to discover a balance between giving and receiving. Between the pleasure of giving and the happiness of receiving.

Knowing how to give before receiving and giving without expecting anything in return belongs to the path that leads to happiness.

Time, money, love or objects, when you give to a person, do it without asking anything in return. Do not expect to receive the same thing in return, neither from the person to whom you give, nor from anyone.

The good news is that life is well done and that she knows how to give, too, unconditionally. And that everyone on earth makes one day or another the experience.

Give a lot. Give little. But always give.

Give, and it will be given to you: one will pour into your breast a good measure, tight, shaken and overflowing; for they will measure you with the measure you have used.

Give and you will always receive the right reward for what you have done. There is more happiness to give than to receive.

When one feels forced to give, it does not provide joy. However, when we give because we really want to give, we find happiness.

Happiness is not only in the generous gesture that is defined as giving everything in exchange for nothing.

To receive is also a right, it is a necessity that gives breath to the heart and builds the essential pillars of reciprocity.

Learning to experience pleasure and the joy of receiving is helpful, since it is a gesture of generosity.

Why? In this way you allow the person giving you to experience his own worth; you give him the opportunity to give and perceive the happiness of giving.

Admitting to receive is a practice that benefits everyone; you have the gaiety to receive a present and the person who offers it, that of making you happy.

Admitting to receive is then giving-giving.

Giving and receiving is part of the balance of human energy that allows harmony in one's work, relationships and environment.

What does giving and receiving mean? This means that most experiences in the world operate on the basis of an exchange, it is essential that you give something to receive later.

For example, if you want to receive love, respect, friendship, etc. You must give the same to others, acquire an item that you must pay, that you have to work.

The earth is always ready to answer you when you sow and take care of your plants.

Sometimes the companies that earn the most money are wrongly criticized, we have to ask ourselves (how much do these companies give to society?).

It is clear that they offer a lot; even some go a bit further thanks to a great social responsibility.

If you give with love and open your heart to receive, then you will find happiness. Giving with love means feeling great joy at doing things well, having a great spirit of service, acting selflessly, maintaining a good attitude most of the time.

If you act with a lot of love, then your heart will be open to receiving and you will enjoy a great balance.

If all the time you do not give and almost never receive, then you will feel an imbalance and it will be a clear message of low self-esteem.

When you give the right to receive and you must demand it, as is the case when buying a product, if you notice that something is wrong, you make the corresponding request, of course to polite way.

People who give only do not fulfill their mission adequately, because they encourage egoism in others. Look at the houses where the mother usually becomes the slave of others, it is inadequate.

It is clear that giving is joy, but if you go to the extreme, then you will never have time to give yourself and receive others.

If you only receive, it's also inappropriate, because you do not trade your energy and you acquire internal debt, which you will have to pay later, a clear example of corruption and illicit activities, some people enrich by these means, but what happens to this money?

It usually disappears quickly and people are in a bad situation again. The answer is clear, they enjoyed an energy they had not paid.

That is why one of the foundations of wealth is to make adequate use of energy, trying at all times to give much more than we expect to receive, so the conviction of abundance will be overwhelming.

Seek to give and receive so that the creative flow is manifested in you.

Look closely at nature, living things give and receive, so it happens with plants and all animals, this balance allows the creative flow to continue to express itself, with the human being the same thing happens, if you want to achieve greatness apply this principle of nature.

The third spiritual law of success is the law of giving. We could also call it the law of giving and receiving because the universe works through a dynamic exchange. Nothing is static.

Our body is in dynamic and constant exchange with the body of the universe; our mind maintains a dynamic interaction with the spirit of the cosmos; our energy is an expression of the energy of the cosmos.

The universe works through a dynamic exchange. Giving and receiving are different aspects of the flow of energy in the universe. And if we are willing to give what we seek, we will keep the abundance of the universe flowing through our lives.

The responsibility to put the Law in motion is ours and it has to be understood that to move freely in our experience, we must first see ourselves as donors.

It can mean a complete change in how we view life, because we often believe that our prosperity depends more on receiving than giving. But for the honest person, life is a process of giving.

Being a donor is an attitude towards life. There are many ways in which we can continue to give.

To be a donor is to know that life is not only about acquiring and taking; it is the satisfying consciousness that our goal is to express.

When you do your job well, without thinking about whether they pay you well or badly, you do your best.

But if you only think about receiving the check and do the minimum possible (under the pretext that you are underpaid), you just take it.

Whenever I meet someone, I will wish them in silence, joy, happiness and well-being.

Sometimes we can think: But what benefit will I draw? When we give the best of ourselves, we activate the

Law of Giving and Receiving and by this law we must receive the best of the Universe.

If we give as little as possible, life will give us the least possible. And if we give to others with love and receive others with gratitude, our good will come back multiplied, it is the Law.

Generally, there are two types of people in life: those who give and those who receive.

Those who receive are people who believe that their life will always be the sum of what they can accumulate in the world.

They always think about acquisition, acquisition, acquisition. They always think of ways to get more money, love, happiness and all kinds of good, but no matter how much they get, they rarely come to know peace and satisfaction.

Those who give, on the other hand, are convinced that life is a process of giving. Therefore, it motivates them to give with love, with a spirit of service, to be helpful, to help as much as possible.

They always feel safe because they intuitively know that good flows from within.

The flow of life is nothing but the harmonious interaction of all the elements and forces that structure the field of existence. This harmonious interaction of the elements and forces of life operates through the law of giving.

Since our body, our mind and the universe maintain a constant and dynamic exchange, slowing down the flow of energy is slowing down the flow of blood.

When the blood stops circulating, it begins to coagulate and stagnate.

Therefore, we must give and receive in order to maintain the wealth and the absence or all that we want in life, circulating constantly.

The word absence comes from the Latin root afuere meaning to flow to. The word absence means "flow in abundance".

Money is really a symbol of the vital energy we exchange, and the vital energy we use as a consequence of the service we give to the universe. Money is also called currency, a name that also reflects the fluid nature of energy.

The word "current" comes from the Latin word "cúrrele" which means running or fleeing.

So if we stop the flow of money, if our only intention is to monopolize the money and hang on to it, we will also prevent, since money is a vital energy that it is circulating again in our life.

In order for this energy to flow constantly towards us, we must keep it in circulation.

Like a river, money must remain in motion, otherwise it begins to stagnate, clog, choke and strangle its own vital force. The traffic keeps you alive and vital.

Every relationship is a relationship of giving and receiving. To give begets to receive, and to receive to give. What goes up must come down; what goes away must come back.

In reality, receiving is the same as giving, because giving and receiving are different aspects of the flow of energy in the universe.

And if we stop the flow of one of the two, we impede the intelligence of nature.

In every seed is the promise of thousands of forests. But the seed must not be hoarded; she must give her intelligence to the fertile soil.

Through his giving action, his invisible energy flows to become a material manifestation.

The more we give, the more we will receive, because we will keep the abundance of the universe in circulation in our life. In reality, all that has value in life multiplies only when it is given.

Which is not multiplied by giving, giving value, or deserving to be received. If in giving we feel that we have lost something, the gift has not been given in reality, and then it will not generate abundance.

When we give reluctantly, there is no energy behind our act of giving.

Life is paradoxical, it asks you to learn to give just what you long for and that will come to you, sooner or later, unsuspectedly, in the least expected way, but in the end it will come.

And if that does not come to your life, it means that life has better plans for you.

In giving and receiving, the most important thing is intention.

The intention must always be to create happiness for the one who gives and the one who receives, because happiness holds and sustains life and, consequently, generates abundance.

The retribution is directly proportional to what is given, when the act is unconditional and comes from the heart.

Therefore, the act of giving must be joyful, the mental attitude must be such that one feels joy in the very act of giving. In this way, the energy that is giving increases several more times.

In reality, practicing the law of giving is very simple. If we want joy, let us give joy to others; if we want love, let us learn to give love; if we desire attention and appreciation, we learn to pay attention and appreciate others; If we want material wealth, help others to reach that wealth.

In fact, the easiest way to get what we want is to help others get what they want.

This principle works for people, businesses, societies and nations alike. If we want to receive the benefit of all the good things in life, let us learn to silently wish the world all the good things in life.

Even the simple idea of giving, the simple desire, or a simple prayer, have the power to affect others.

It is because our body, reduced to its essential state, is an individual beam of energy and information within a universe of energy and information.

We are individual bundles of consciousness within a conscious universe. The word consciousness implies much more than energy and information, involves energy and information that live in the form of thought.

Therefore, we are beams of thought in the middle of a thinking universe. And thought has the power to transform.

Life is the eternal dance of consciousness, manifested as a dynamic exchange of intelligence impulses between the microcosm and the macrocosm, between the human body and the universal body, between the human mind and the cosmic spirit.

When we learn to give what we seek, we activate this dance and its choreography with an exquisite, energetic and vital movement that constitutes the eternal beating of life.

The best way to put the law to work, to initiate the whole process of movement, is to make the decision that whenever we come in contact with someone, we will give them something.

They do not have to be material things; it could be a flower, a compliment or a prayer. In reality, the most powerful means of giving are not material.

Gifts such as interest, attention, affection, appreciation and love are among the most valuable that can be given, and they cost nothing.

When we meet someone, silently send him a wish for his joy, happiness and well-being. This form of silent generosity is very powerful.

One of the things that was taught to me in my childhood, and that I also want to teach my children, is never to visit someone without bringing something, we never visit someone without giving him a gift.

However, one might ask: How can I give gifts to others if now I do not even have enough for me?

We can give a flower; only one flower. We can bring a note or a card that expresses something about our feelings towards the person we are visiting.

We can bring a compliment. We can bring a prayer.

Let's take the decision to give wherever we go, and to whomever we see. As we give, we will receive. The more we give, the more we will trust the miraculous effects of this law. And as we receive more, our ability to give increases.

Our true nature is that of prosperity and abundance; we are naturally prosperous because nature comes to all needs and desires.

We lack nothing because our essential nature is pure potentiality, infinite possibilities.

Therefore, we must know that we are already intrinsically wealthy, regardless of how much money we have, because the source of all wealth is the field of pure potentiality is the consciousness that knows how to satisfy every need, including joy, I love, laughter, peace, harmony and knowledge.

If we seek these things first, not only for ourselves, but for others, everything else will spontaneously come to us.

Now, I give well of myself, my talents, my money, my compassion. I give with love and without ties, and I receive with gratitude and freely, and that's how it is.

We must always make a habit of giving with joy. Give before receiving. Whatever type of energy you are going to transform in an incredible way.

You can give your time, for example, and it will come much later from an unexpected source, in an unexpected way and in a way that benefits you immensely.

You cannot insist on a particular form and time in which you will come back, but you can be sure that it will come back to you in the best way.

Give, give, give. And we must give freely and with joy.

It is the energy behind what matters so do not give up reluctantly. The law of cause and effect ensures that you will receive what you give.

Life is to give. Give what you have of your time, money, smiles, love, compliments, anything and you will receive what you do not have with you. Give with luxury and receive grateful.

Grace and gratitude are energizing factors of giving and receiving.

By taking care of society and nature, you take care of yourself. Share and give often to nature and to society.

Help others in the proportion and the point where you bring others to build their wealth so that you can build your own. The universe is all energy. The energy flows.

Giving favors this flow of energy by putting you in harmony with the powers of the universe.

For whatever you want, have another being first and you will start having it in abundance. Give and you will receive multiplied.

Develop an awareness that allows you to be attentive and see all the opportunities where you can give something freely and happily.

You can give material and immaterial things, your time, your skills or anything else.

Get rid of the habit of thinking that you should receive before giving. That's not giving, it's exchanging.

Giving freely and happily allows you to do business, if you want to look that way, with the universe.

That's how it works; you give something you have with someone with freedom and joy. The universe, by the law, finds the best way to return this energy to you in the form of something you do not have with you.

It is yours, when it is the most appropriate time in the most appropriate way. It's a magic process.

Obviously, the more you give, the more you create magic for yourself. Life begins to work for you.

Develop a strong desire and persistence to give joyfully and freely.

When setting goals, be sure to include several goals that include giving freely and happily. Giving, under the law of cause and effect, is one of the most powerful actions you can take.

Returns in multiples, seven times. You cannot let yourself go by giving up your plan of life. You can not let this happen at random.

Develop the fact of giving until it is a habit, something you do naturally without having to think about it. It makes you a persistent and consistent donor and the universe works for you.

Give spontaneously. Work with the habit of giving until you have the pleasure of giving. Enjoy it completely.

It is good to think and know that when you give, you will get something from the universe.

You do not have to pretend that you are not interested in receiving a reward for giving. It is good to wait for a reward. In fact, waiting for a reward gives the power to the reward to come to you.

The reward you receive will come from a source, at a time and in a way that the universe will find what suits you best. You always have something to give. Time, praise, talent, money, knowledge, sharing and your knowledge, etc.

Giving an extra reward effect, it shows you what you have, but you did not know you had it. Help where you can with this knowledge, share this kind of knowledge.

You are surrounded by abundant opportunities to give but you only see them when you decide to start seeing them. Also learn to receive abundantly and happily.

Do not feel uncomfortable receiving. You deserve it and you are in harmony with the law of giving and receiving.

Offer your gift for free and with joy. Show your hand. Do not push.

Show. If the recipient does not want to take your gift, respect it with joy. Do not be offended if your gift is not accepted.

Allow the other person to fully utilize the nature of the freedom of choice and not make the person dependent on you.

When a person becomes unnecessarily dependent on your gifts, you do him no favors because you reduce his belief and ability in himself.

Here we have a probable scenario. Imagine someone who does not have a lot of material things to give and share with others, but who is a very kind and charming person.

Give thousands of compliments to people who show up without receiving them.

Raise spirit and confidence by finding ways to encourage and flatter, but never receive compliments from anyone. Very good, do not worry. The universe keeps its accounts perfectly.

The gift of this person accumulates credit in the universal system. One day, according to the law of cause and effect, to give and receive, the person receives in one way or another the object that he always wanted to have when he needed it, a which seems like a miracle.

You give only a little when you give your possessions. It's when you give yourself that you really give. What are possessions, if not things, that you keep in fear that you need them tomorrow?

What is fear of necessity if not fear in itself? Is it not the fear of thirst when your well is full of insatiable thirst?

There are those who give little of what they have and give it to gain recognition but their hidden desire makes the gift unhealthy. And there are those who have little and who give everything.

Keeping all other things constant, an individual or a society will attain wealth and happiness to the extent that they share and give in the right way.

Now, so to speak, you know how to do business with the universe. The universe itself is a universe of giving because life is to be given. You give and receive seven times, you are really rewarded for your kindness.

The Source, the Life, is all about giving and the Intelligence that governs the universe always respects your giving action, always in every way.

Give with joy! Everything in life is a gift. Especially in relation to wealth and happiness, never stop making others have wealth and happiness and you will have wealth and happiness.

But what is good to give? To receive. And what's going on with that? Gratitude.

Consciously using the power of gratitude, this is an extremely important aspect to attract to you the abundance and happiness you desire and deserve in your life.

First, let's explore the sincerity of gratitude in a strictly scientific perspective and how, through our individual choices to develop a constant habit of expressing our deep gratitude, it promulgates the unshakeable power of UNIVERSAL LAW to attract more than to thank.

As we have discovered in the law of vibration, all that is in our universe divided in its purest form is a vibrating mass of atoms and subatomic particles.

Thanks to the law of attraction, the energy (vibrations) that resonates and the project based on your thoughts, feelings and emotions that determines your vibratory frequency emission frequencies, attracts the frequencies of energy or vibration that harmonize or resonate with what determines the events, situations and circumstances that appeal to you and ultimately manifest in your life.

To ensure this harmonious relationship, it is of supreme and vital importance that I should give a place to your discussion here and give you instructions that, if you follow them, they will surely unite you in thought with supreme power.

I will put the law into effect by committing myself to do the following:

1) I will bring a gift wherever I go and for everyone with whom I am. This gift can be a compliment, a flower or a prayer. Today, I will give something to everyone I meet, to start spreading the joy, wealth and prosperity in my life and the lives of others.

2) Today, I will receive with gratitude all the gifts that life gives me. I will receive the gifts of nature, sunlight and song of birds, or the spring showers or the first snows of winter.

    I will also be open to receiving others, be it a material gift, money, a compliment or a prayer.

3) I am committed to keep plenty in circulation by giving and receiving the most precious gifts of life: affection, affection, appreciation and love. Whenever I meet someone, I wish them happiness, happiness and well-being in silence.

CHAPTER 17

BECOME FINANCIALLY FREE

When someone is told that he or she is financially free, it usually means that the person has huge savings or income from his or her investments, and therefore has peace of mind with regard to their financial life. .

So, she gets the satisfaction of being able to do what she wants as she wants to do. Financial freedom contributes to a greater sense of general freedom, it means being able to enjoy life and live your life as you see fit.

On the other hand, when people are under financial pressure, they usually suffer from stress, anxiety and even relationship problems. Financial freedom reduces or eliminates these negative consequences. As I say, money does not make happiness, but it contributes to it. In reality, the whole notion of financial freedom revolves around two essential factors, money and time.

Being financially free means having enough money to be able to spend your time on things you really want to do. But most of the time, we spend most of our day doing things we do not really want to, but we have to do it.

Of course, for a large number of people, a serious dimension is freedom from work. Whether you are an employee or a self-employed person, the hard truth is that you have to create money to be able to eat, to lodge and to pay your debts. For many people, there is no other choice.

The employee is forced to go to work daily, and his only hope of becoming free one day is retirement. And the job, it takes a lot of our time. And more beautiful, if we see the time spent in the trips to go.

On the other hand, to have the goal of building financial freedom is to hope for time for yourself.

To have time to dedicate oneself to one's passions, be it to adopt an art, to adopt a sport, to make trips, to work on social or religious actions, etc ... It is to choose to fulfill one's dreams and to to be able to do what you want when you want. And especially having the resources to do it means having the time and the financial means.

Financial Freedom is not necessarily the same as becoming rich. Of course, achieving financial freedom includes having enough financial resources to maintain one's lifestyle. However, that does not mean you have to be a billionaire to access it. It all depends on how you live.

Someone who just wants a modest life, and who does not like luxury goods, will be able to achieve financial freedom with reasonable capital.

To be financially free, you need time, money and energy. First, you have money so you can buy what you want, live life on your own terms. Have time to devote to what matters to you.

If you earn a lot of money yet never have time for the people you love or realize what matters to you, and finally, have vitality, health, energy; What's its use?

To speak specifically of financial freedom, one must approach two different but complementary concepts.

Of course, one could designate financial freedom as being just in a way of administering one's money that would lead to no longer being under the tutelage of anybody, or the arrival of one's pay check or salary.

In other words, one could define financial freedom as a broader concept, a complete conception of one's lifestyle which would obviously lead one to no longer be at the mercy of anyone else except oneself. What has to do with the money, the management of its savings?

How to achieve financial freedom?

To be financially free, you must exist according to a unique truth, which was already well learned by our ancestors: Spend less than you earn.

When we receive money, we are always tempted to waste it, make new purchases, projects, travel, neglecting the necessary, your savings. Save it is to contribute to your fortune tomorrow, to the construction of a capital of great value.

If you pay off all the money you receive, you try to experience difficulties. For example if you have unforeseen expenses (such as repairs to your car), you will have to borrow to pay them. People who live this way are regularly stressed about money.

If you spend more money than you receive, then you are certainly in trouble. People who live in this way are in a condition of incessant calamity.

When we receive our pay, we tend to shell out without actually claiming the reason and effect of our action. This behavior will be harmful to us if our goal is to achieve financial freedom.

Conversely, we must distinguish what is primordial and what is imperative from what is not. If it is also in your customs, then neglect everything in the last class so that you can keep your money for the most useful.

You will know that you will have to buy something when the other one will be almost unusable or lost while you usually need it.

You will also have to think of another choice, a less expensive issue, if you were to buy an expensive product.

In particular prohibit you to generate new necessities and keep only the necessary, otherwise it will make you waste time and money while the goal is to pick up. You will hold this freedom at the end of this program that you have determined.

Currently, with credit cards and payment facilities, it is very simple and very attractive to live on top of one's resources. A lot of people, of course, spend more than they earn, and do not even realize that they are running into disaster.

If you want to become financially free, first you must free yourself from your debts. Get rid of it, by all possible legal means. Look for another job with better pay, if you find that your present financial capacity will not allow you this release.

In the ideal, when everything will be erased, erase now the borrowing of your customs and try to get out every time with what you own.

Become aware of your income as your expenses. And since outings are almost always more than income, you need to deal with them more effectively. To do so, organize all your expenses and keep a budget for everyone.

They will be called the envelopes, one for the expenses of the house, another for the food, another for the transport, another for the studies if you make some, another for the various refunds or the debts if you still have some etc. You obviously have the right to also have an envelope for your little fantasies and your hobbies; however you should tighten your belt if you want to arrive safely from your challenge.

Calculate, however do not proceed according to your wishes, since you cannot grant it yet. Put only the small essentials in these envelopes and you will be able to see what is left over. Place a small margin if you want, however be fair with yourself.

Make savings every month if you want to live in financial freedom later. Take this savings as soon as you receive your pay before distributing the rest in the envelopes.

This money you can use later, especially by investments. It will expand if you take it seriously. Your savings then stems from your payroll, to which you will have removed your budget which should already honor the first principle, the prioritization of expenses.

In any project, you need a program, normally relative to the chronology to be able to note the progress or the delays in the duration.

You must clarify all the points that are attached to your budget. When are you attacking and by what? How much do you have to spend monthly and how much should it stay in your bank account? What will you invest in later?

Obviously, there may be permutations en route, however, make sure that they are constantly well studied, it is for this reason the influx of boundaries is important.

You must also schedule for when you will generate or complete your capital, and how much you want to earn for this year and for the following years. An exact plan, to be followed word for word, is essential.

I am particularly speaking to people of more or less low income, however who have a great dream, they are advised to increase their income. To access them, they will have to take advantage of the various investments that will increase their money.

They can also invest in the incalculable economic sectors, examining those that are pleasant in their community. And of course, these people will be able to start looking for a job that could earn them more than before.

Keeping your money warm will not lead very far. You have to run the risk of investing them, and there are not the options that are missing. It will be essential at this level to be competent in the field to be able to catch the opportunities that arise, to be able to grow quickly its capital and stop the loss of money. Investigate the real estate sector, land, pharmaceutical industry, new technologies, etc.

The most intrepid can start on the stock market. Also possible, the acquisition of shares in large companies, however it will be for when you have raised enough money, since the necessary amount will be very high. Otherwise, there is the Internet and the many doors it has opened for successful activities.

There is no better alternative to achieving true financial freedom than setting up your own business.

Competition is important wherever you go, unless you offer innovative products or satisfy needs that have not yet been examined. You can also generate new ones. In other words, you will need to be imaginative and authentic.

Do not think that the market is saturated; take symbol on those who have just appeared. Hear their story and generate yours. In life, know that anything is possible.

Who knows if instead of sticking to a consistent financial freedom you become richer? And then, if you want to stop working, you can give up your business to absolutely enjoy the money that it has allowed you to earn.

However, do not sleep on these dreams, you must think, imagine, work, study and stand up before you get there.

Implementing all these instructions involves a big task that will undoubtedly take place over many years. Arm yourself with this audacity, tenacity and do not leave the lens of the eyes or preferably your thoughts.

Allow yourself to work courageously and you will see the result of your efforts appear gradually and later stride. Make trips and communicate with each other to see how others are doing and to see where you can make the most of your career path.

Develop a good program every time you enter a market or a specific stage, learn more daily to refine yourself and prevent scams, learn from your mistakes and develop your armor if the result takes time to be felt.

Never give up in order not to regret. And again, be constantly positive and always take care of your health.

If you have any capacity, it's time to take it into account and enjoy it, since a large number of people have certainly arrived in this direction, painter, writer, singer, producer, etc. So, you will be able to live off your talents by selling your jobs. At this point, it would definitely be financial independence as you have total control over your income and expenses.

And when you have gained a large sum, you need not be obstinate. Enjoy life and inevitably enjoy every moment. Do everything you ever wanted to do before. Know how to use your free time, especially if you have stopped working, especially by taking care of yourself and your loved ones.

Convenience and well-being should be more affordable at that time.

Financial freedom is built gradually and programmed. First, it is to build income that will take over the money that came from the wage. However, we must also think about the long term and have a well-established program.

Of course, the one who chooses to leave the security of a salaried job to live his dream, must reflect on the scale of his entire existence. Above all, he must ensure that he will continue to have an income when he is old, and have social assistance to cover the cost of health.

On the other hand, we must not forget to think about the indeterminate costs of raising children. In conclusion, it is prediction and understanding that help to be truly free of money problems.

However, do not think that this only concerns some rare people. Everyone should think about building financial independence.

Even if you do not stop working, the economic and financial crises that we are experiencing surely have shown you how ephemeral job stability is. Everything can happen, and no one is safe from an unforeseen event.

I think it is the responsibility of every individual to expand his financial independence as much as he can, and not rely on the assistance of his government.

Therefore, to access financial freedom, you need to have sources of income other than employment. This is called passive income and alternative income.

Passive income, unlike active income, is money you earn without sacrificing your time. While the majority of people turn their time into money (a salary), there are individuals who generate wealth from many sources of passive income.

These people receive money 24 hours a day, 7 days a week, and the money appears on their bank account even while they are sleeping or while traveling. If you are looking for independence financial freedom, you must learn to think and act like them, in order to set up a set of passive income.

In reality, there is little income that is completely passive, except the interest that gives money back into a bank account and investment in furniture. However, in almost every other case, there is some work to be done at one time or another, if only to make the investment choice and inspect it.

However, when we talk about passive income, that is to say, these revenues are loosened from the time spent on them.

Real estate is a good source of passive income and, personally, it is my favorite. Every month, you receive rent and your job is spent watching your bank account to see that the money has been deposited. However, when there are repairs to be made, or a tenant chooses to leave, we must sacrifice a little time. Fortunately, it's rare.

Alternative income is any other source of income generated by an activity that is not the main work. It can take all the forms you want, and especially the creation of a company. In this area, the internet offers possibilities that did not exist until recently.

It is perfectly possible to design one or more internet sites that bring back money. The site can sell 24 hours a day, even during your sleep.

In reality, you will truly be free only if you make financial independence a major vision of your life, and you make efforts to make it happen. The question is what do you really want, spend your money now to get the latest fashionable gadget, or save and invest.

The majority of people who have achieved financial freedom made short-term sacrifices to earn long-term profits when they were building the foundation of their fortunes.

Not only do they invest a proportionally huge share of their income, but they resist the desire to waste what their investments bring back to them. Finally, the most useful is the ability to give the advantage to the investment of preference rather than to spend.

Having the goal of having passive income that makes you receive money even while you sleep, does not mean you do not have to work hard. In fact, unlike active income (salary), you may have to work so hard, and possibly even harder, to set up a source of passive income.

However, the profits will be much larger, once you have designed a source of passive income, it will continue to work for you, even when you stop working. On the other hand, income from an activity stops as long as you stop working.

To design a source of passive income, then you must be available to work hard to make it happen. However, once the device reaches its cruising speed, you will not have to worry about it until sometimes and you can dedicate yourself to your passions.